ALL QUIET ON THE WESTERN FRONT

Erich Maria Remarque

SPARK PUBLISHIN

This Spark Publishing edition 2014 by SparkNotes LLC, an Affiliate of Barnes & Noble

122 Fifth Avenue
New York, NY 10011
www.sparknotes.com

ISBN 978-1-4114-6941-9

Please submit changes or report errors to www.sparknotes.com/errors.

Printed in Canada

10 9 8 7 6 5 4 3

Contents

CONTEXT

ERICH MARIA REMARQUE WAS BORN IN OSNABRÜCK, Germany, in 1898 into a lower-middle-class family. In 1916, he was drafted into the German army to fight in World War I, in which he was badly wounded. Ten years after the war ended, he published *Im Westen Nichts Neues,* translated into English a year later as *All Quiet on the Western Front,* a novel about the experiences of ordinary German soldiers during the war.

Though other books, most notably Stephen Crane's *The Red Badge of Courage* (1895), had explored the violence and brutality of war in a realistic light, the literary tradition of war stories still tended overwhelmingly toward romanticized ideals of glory, adventure, and honor. In presenting his grimly realistic version of a soldier's experience, Remarque stripped the typical romanticism from the war narrative in the staunchly antiwar *All Quiet on the Western Front.* The novel instantly became an international, critically acclaimed success. An American movie based on the book was released in 1930.

After Adolf Hitler's rise to power in Germany in the early 1930s, the fiercely nationalistic Nazi regime attacked *All Quiet on the Western Front* and Remarque as unpatriotic. Remarque made no attempt to resist the Nazis' attacks on his reputation because he feared retaliation. Despite Nazi hostilities toward him, in 1931 Remarque published a sequel to *All Quiet on the Western Front*, entitled *The Road Back,* which details the postwar experience of German citizens. This work provoked further Nazi opposition, and Remarque fled to Switzerland with his wife, Jutta Zambona, in 1932. In 1933, the Nazis banned Remarque's two novels and held a bonfire to burn copies of the books.

Remarque and his wife divorced in Switzerland but eventually remarried so that she could retain her Swiss residency. In 1939, he followed the path of many persecuted German intellectuals and immigrated to the United States, where he obtained citizenship in 1947. His family was not so lucky: the Nazis killed his sister during World War II, in part because of her relationship to him. Remarque and his wife had separated; in 1951, they finally ended their estranged marriage.

In the Unites States, Remarque had a tempestuous affair with the actress Marlene Dietrich, which inspired his novel *Arch of Triumph*. In 1958, he married another film star, Paulette Goddard. They eventually left the United States and moved to Porto Ranco, Switzerland, where Remarque died on September 25, 1970.

Most of Remarque's novels deal with political and social upheaval in Europe during the First and Second World Wars. Several of his novels were adapted to film. However, *All Quiet on the Western Front* remains his masterpiece; none of his other works approaches its critical acclaim and popularity. The novel and its first film adaptation are still influential as antiwar works and important chronicles of World War I. One of the remarkable aspects of the book's success in England and America is that, unlike most other works dealing with World War I, *All Quiet on the Western Front* deals with the experiences of German soldiers—detested enemies of the English and Americans during World War I and World War II. That American and English reception of the book was so positive from the outset testifies to its ability to speak for all soldiers who suffered through the horrors of World War I.

Plot Overview

All Quiet on the Western Front is narrated by Paul Bäumer, a young man of nineteen who fights in the German army on the French front in World War I. Paul and several of his friends from school joined the army voluntarily after listening to the stirring patriotic speeches of their teacher, Kantorek. But after experiencing ten weeks of brutal training at the hands of the petty, cruel Corporal Himmelstoss and the unimaginable brutality of life on the front, Paul and his friends have realized that the ideals of nationalism and patriotism for which they enlisted are simply empty clichés. They no longer believe that war is glorious or honorable, and they live in constant physical terror.

When Paul's company receives a short reprieve after two weeks of fighting, only eighty men of the original 150-man company return from the front. The cook doesn't want to give the survivors the rations that were meant for the dead men but eventually agrees to do so; the men thus enjoy a large meal. Paul and his friends visit Kemmerich, a former classmate who has recently had a leg amputated after contracting gangrene. Kemmerich is slowly dying, and Müller, another former classmate, wants Kemmerich's boots for himself. Paul doesn't consider Müller insensitive; like the other soldiers, Müller simply realizes pragmatically that Kemmerich no longer needs his boots. Surviving the agony of war, Paul observes, forces one to learn to disconnect oneself from emotions like grief, sympathy, and fear. Not long after this encounter, Paul returns to Kemmerich's bedside just as the young man dies. At Kemmerich's request, Paul takes his boots to Müller.

A group of new recruits comes to reinforce the company, and Paul's friend Kat produces a beef and bean stew that impresses them. Kat says that if all the men in an army, including the officers, were paid the same wage and given the same food, wars would be over immediately. Kropp, another of Paul's former classmates, says that there should be no armies; he argues that a nation's leaders should instead fight out their disagreements with clubs. They discuss the fact that petty, insignificant people become powerful and arrogant during war, and Tjaden, a member of Paul's company, announces that the cruel Corporal Himmelstoss has come to fight at the front.

At night, the men go on a harrowing mission to lay barbed wire at the front. Pounded by artillery, they hide in a graveyard, where the force of the shelling causes the buried corpses to emerge from their graves, as groups of living men fall dead around them. After this gruesome event, the surviving soldiers return to their camp, where they kill lice and think about what they will do at the end of the war. Some of the men have tentative plans, but all of them seem to feel that the war will never end. Paul fears that if the war did end, he wouldn't know what to do with himself. Himmelstoss arrives at the front; when the men see him, Tjaden insults him. The men's lieutenant gives them light punishment but also lectures Himmelstoss about the futility of saluting at the front. Paul and Kat find a house with a goose and roast the goose for supper, enjoying a rare good meal.

The company is caught in a bloody battle with a charging group of Allied infantrymen. Men are blown apart, limbs are severed from torsos, and giant rats pick at the dead and the wounded. Paul feels that he must become an animal in battle, trusting only his instincts to keep him alive. After the battle, only thirty-two of eighty men are still alive. The men are given a short reprieve at a field depot. Paul and some of his friends go for a swim, which ends in a rendezvous with a group of French girls. Paul desperately wishes to recapture his innocence with a girl, but he feels that it is impossible to do so.

Paul receives seventeen days of leave and goes home to see his family. He feels awkward and oppressed in his hometown, unable to discuss his traumatic experiences with anyone. He learns that his mother is dying of cancer and that Kantorek has been conscripted as a soldier, from which he derives a certain cold satisfaction. He visits Kemmerich's mother and tells her, untruthfully, that her son's death was instant and painless. At the end of his leave, Paul spends some time at a training camp near a group of Russian prisoners-of-war. Paul feels that the Russians are people just like him, not subhuman enemies, and wonders how war can make enemies of people who have no grudge against one another.

Paul is sent back to his company and is reunited with his friends. The kaiser, the German emperor, pays a visit to the front, and the men are disappointed to see that he is merely a short man with a weak voice. In battle, Paul is separated from his company and forced to hide in a shell hole. A French soldier jumps into the shell hole with him, and Paul instinctively stabs him. As the man dies a slow, painful death, Paul is overcome with remorse for having hurt him. He feels again that this enemy soldier is no enemy at all but rather a victim of war just like himself. Paul looks through the soldier's things and finds that his name was Gérard Duval and learns that Duval had a wife and child at home. When he returns to his company, Paul recounts the incident to his friends, who try to console him.

Paul and his friends are given an easy assignment: for three weeks, they are to guard a supply depot away from the fighting. When the next battle takes place, Paul and Kropp are wounded and forced to bribe a sergeant-major with cigars in order to be placed on the hospital train together. At the hospital, Paul undergoes surgery. Kropp's leg is amputated, and he becomes extremely depressed. After his surgery, Paul has a short leave at home before he returns to his company.

As the German army begins to give in to the unrelenting pressure of the Allied forces, Paul's friends are killed in combat one by one. Detering, one of Paul's close friends, attempts to desert but is caught and court-martialed. Kat is killed when a piece of shrapnel slices his head open while Paul is carrying him to safety. By the fall of 1918, Paul is the only one of his circle of friends who is still alive. Soldiers everywhere whisper that the Germans will soon surrender and that peace will come. Paul is poisoned in a gas attack and given a short leave. He reflects that, when the war ends, he will be ruined for peacetime; all he knows is the war. In October 1918, on a day with very little fighting, Paul is killed. The army report for that day reads simply: "All quiet on the Western Front." Paul's corpse wears a calm expression, as though relieved that the end has come at last.

Character List

Paul Bäumer A young German soldier fighting in the trenches during World War I. Paul is the protagonist and narrator of the novel. He is, at heart, a kind, compassionate, and sensitive young man, but the brutal experience of warfare teaches him to detach himself from his feelings. His account of the war is a bitter invective against sentimental, romantic ideals of warfare.

Stanislaus Katczinsky A soldier belonging to Paul's company and Paul's best friend in the army. Kat, as he is known, is forty years old at the beginning of the novel and has a family at home. He is a resourceful, inventive man and always finds food, clothing, and blankets whenever he and his friends need them.

Albert Kropp One of Paul's classmates who serves with Paul in the Second Company. An intelligent, speculative young man, Kropp is one of Paul's closest friends during the war. His interest in analyzing the causes of the war leads to many of the most critical antiwar sentiments in the novel.

Müller One of Paul's classmates. Müller is a hardheaded, practical young man, and he plies his friends in the Second Company with questions about their postwar plans.

Tjaden One of Paul's friends in the Second Company. Tjaden is a wiry young man with a voracious appetite. He bears a deep grudge against Corporal Himmelstoss.

Kantorek A pompous, ignorant, authoritarian schoolmaster in Paul's high school during the years before the war. Kantorek places intense pressure on Paul and his classmates to fulfill their "patriotic duty" by enlisting in the army.

Corporal Himmelstoss A noncommissioned training officer. Before the war, Himmelstoss was a postman. He is a petty, power-hungry little man who torments Paul and his friends during their training. After he experiences the horrors of trench warfare, however, he tries to make amends with them.

Franz Kemmerich One of Paul's classmates and comrades in the war. After suffering a light wound, Kemmerich contracts gangrene, and his leg has to be amputated. His death, in Chapter Two, marks the reader's first encounter with the meaninglessness of death and the cheapness of life in the war.

Joseph Behm The first of Paul's classmates to die in the war. Behm did not want to enlist, but he caved under the pressure of the schoolmaster, Kantorek. His ugly, painful death shatters his classmates' trust in the authorities who convinced them to take part in the war.

Detering One of Paul's close friends in the Second Company. Detering is a young man with a wife and a farm at home; he is constantly homesick for his farm and family.

Gérard Duval A French soldier whom Paul kills in No Man's Land. Duval is a printer with a wife and child at home. He is the first person that Paul kills in hand-to-hand combat, one of Paul's most traumatic experiences in the war.

Leer One of Paul's classmates and close friends during the war. Leer serves with Paul in the Second Company. He was the first in Paul's class to lose his virginity.

Haie Westhus One of Paul's friends in the Second Company. A gigantic, burly man, Westhus was a peat-digger before the war. He plans to serve a full term in the army after the war ends, since he finds peat-digging so unpleasant.

Kindervater A soldier in a neighboring unit. Kindervater is a bed wetter like Tjaden.

Lewandowski A patient in the Catholic hospital where Paul and Kropp recuperate from their wounds. Lewandowski desperately wants to have sex with his visiting wife but is confined to bed because of a minor fever.

Mittelstaedt One of Paul's classmates. Mittelstaedt becomes a training officer and enjoys tormenting Kantorek when Kantorek is conscripted as a soldier.

Analysis of Major Characters

Paul Bäumer

As the novel's narrator and protagonist, Paul is the central figure in *All Quiet on the Western Front* and serves as the mouthpiece for Remarque's meditations about war. Throughout the novel, Paul's inner personality is contrasted with the way the war forces him to act and feel. His memories of the time before the war show that he was once a very different man from the despairing soldier who now narrates the novel. Paul is a compassionate and sensitive young man; before the war, he loved his family and wrote poetry. Because of the horror of the war and the anxiety it induces, Paul, like other soldiers, learns to disconnect his mind from his feelings, keeping his emotions at bay in order to preserve his sanity and survive.

As a result, the compassionate young man becomes unable to mourn his dead comrades, unable to feel at home among his family, unable to express his feelings about the war or even talk about his experiences, unable to remember the past fully, and unable to conceive of a future without war. He also becomes a "human animal," capable of relying on animal instinct to kill and survive in battle. But because Paul is extremely sensitive, he is somewhat less able than many of the other soldiers to detach himself completely from his feelings, and there are several moments in the book (Kemmerich's death, Kat's death, the time that he spends with his ill mother) when he feels himself pulled down by emotion. These surging feelings indicate the extent to which war has programmed Paul to cut himself off from feeling, as when he says, with devastating understatement, "Parting from my friend Albert Kropp was very hard. But a man gets used to that sort of thing in the army."

Paul's experience is intended to represent the experience of a whole generation of men, the so-called lost generation—men who went straight from childhood to fighting in World War I, often as adolescents. Paul frequently considers the past and the future from the perspective of his entire generation, noting that, when the war ends, he and his friends will not know what to do, as they have learned to be adults only while fighting the war. The longer that Paul survives the war and the more that he hates it, the less certain he is that life will be better for him after it ends. This anxiety arises from his belief that the war will have ruined his generation, will have so eviscerated his and his friends' minds that they will always be "bewildered." Against such depressing expectations, Paul is relieved by his death: "his face had an expression of calm, as though almost glad the end had come." The war becomes not merely a traumatic experience or a hardship to be endured but something that actually transforms the essence of human existence into irrevocable, endless suffering. The war destroys Paul long before it kills him.

Kantorek

Though he is not central to the novel's plot, Kantorek is an important figure as a focus of Remarque's bitter critique of the ideals of patriotism and nationalism that drove nations into the catastrophe of World War I. Kantorek, the teacher who filled his students' heads with passionate rhetoric about duty and glory, serves as a punching bag as Remarque argues against those ideals. Though a modern context is essential to the indictment of Kantorek's patriotism and nationalism, Kantorek's physical description groups him with premodern evil characters. The fierce and pompous Kantorek is a small man described as "energetic and uncompromising," characteristics that recall the worried Caesar's remarks about Cassius in Shakespeare's *Julius Caesar*: "Yon Cassius has a lean and hungry look. / He thinks too much. Such men are dangerous" (I.ii.195–196). Napoleon also springs to mind as a historical model for Kantorek.

The inclusion of a seemingly anachronistic literary type—the scheming or dangerous diminutive man—may seem out of place in a modern novel. Yet this quality of Kantorek arguably reflects the espousal of dated ideas by an older generation of leaders who betray their followers with manipulations, ignorance, and lies. "While they taught that duty to one's country is the greatest thing," Paul writes in Chapter One, "we already knew that death-throes are stronger." As schoolboys, Paul and his friends believed that Kantorek was an enlightened man whose authority derived from his wisdom; as soldiers, they quickly learn to see through Kantorek's rhetoric and grow to despise him, especially after the death of Joseph Behm. That Kantorek is eventually drafted and makes a terrible soldier reflects the uselessness of the ideals that he touts.

Corporal Himmelstoss

Like Kantorek, Himmelstoss does not figure heavily in the novel's plot, but his thematic importance makes him significant to the book as a whole. One of the themes of *All Quiet on the Western Front* is that war brings out a savagery and hunger for power that lie latent in many people, even if they are normally respectable, nonviolent citizens. Himmelstoss is just such a figure: an unthreatening postman before the war, he evolves into the "terror of Klosterberg," the most feared disciplinarian in the training camps. Himmelstoss is extremely cruel to his recruits, forcing them to obey ridiculous and dangerous orders simply because he enjoys bullying them.

Himmelstoss forces his men to stand outside with no gloves on during a hard frost, risking frostbite that could lead to the amputation of a finger or the loss of a hand. His idea of a cure for Tjaden's bed-wetting—making him share a bunk with Kindervater, another bed wetter—is vicious, especially since the bed-wetting results from a medical condition and is not under Tjaden's control. At this stage of the novel, Himmelstoss represents the meanest, pettiest, most loathsome aspects of humanity that war draws out. But when he is sent to fight at the front, Himmelstoss experiences the same terror and trauma as the other soldiers, and he quickly tries to make amends for his past behavior. In this way, Remarque exhibits the frightening and awesome power of the trenches, which transform even a mad disciplinarian into a terrorized soldier desperate for human companionship.

Themes, Motifs & Symbols

Themes

Themes are the fundamental and often universal ideas explored in a literary work.

The Horror of War

The overriding theme of *All Quiet on the Western Front* is the terrible brutality of war, which informs every scene in the novel. Whereas war novels before *All Quiet on the Western Front* tended to romanticize what war was like, emphasizing ideas such as glory, honor, patriotic duty, and adventure, *All Quiet on the Western Front* sets out to portray war as it was actually experienced, replacing the romantic picture of glory and heroism with a decidedly unromantic vision of fear, meaninglessness, and butchery. In many ways, World War I demanded this depiction more than any war before it—it completely altered mankind's conception of military conflict with its catastrophic levels of carnage and violence, its battles that lasted for months, and its gruesome new technological advancements (e.g., machine guns, poison gas, trenches) that made killing easier and more impersonal than ever before. Remarque's novel dramatizes these aspects of World War I and portrays the mind-numbing terror and savagery of war with a relentless focus on the physical and psychological damage that it occasions. At the end of the novel, almost every major character is dead, epitomizing the war's devastating effect on the generation of young men who were forced to fight it.

The Effect of War on the Soldier

Because *All Quiet on the Western Front* is set among soldiers fighting on the front, one of its main focuses is the ruinous effect that war has on the soldiers who fight it. These men are subject to constant physical danger, as they could literally be blown to pieces at any moment. This intense physical threat also serves as an unceasing attack on the nerves, forcing soldiers to cope with primal, instinctive fear during every waking moment. Additionally, the soldiers are forced to live in appalling conditions—in filthy, waterlogged ditches full of rats and decaying corpses and infested with lice. They frequently go without food and sleep, adequate clothing, or sufficient medical care. They are forced, moreover, to deal with the frequent, sudden deaths of their close friends and comrades, often in close proximity and in extremely violent fashion. Remarque portrays the overall effect of these conditions as a crippling overload of panic and despair. The only way for soldiers to survive is to disconnect themselves from their feelings, suppressing their emotions and accepting the conditions of their lives.

In Remarque's view, this emotional disconnection has a hugely destructive impact on a soldier's humanity; Paul, for instance, becomes unable to imagine a future without the war and unable to remember how he felt in the past. He also loses his ability to speak to his family. Soldiers no longer pause to mourn fallen friends and comrades; when Kemmerich is on his deathbed, at the beginning of the novel, the most pressing question among his friends is who will inherit his boots. Among the living soldiers, however, Remarque portrays intense bonds of loyalty and friendship that spring up as a result of the shared experience of war. These feelings are the only romanticized element of the novel and are virtually the only emotions that preserve the soldiers' fundamental humanity.

Nationalism and Political Power

In many ways, the precipitating cause of World War I was the ethic of nationalism, the idea that competing nation-states were a fundamental part of existence, that one owed one's first loyalty to one's nation, and that one's national identity was the primary component of one's overall identity. The ethic of nationalism was not new, but it had reached new heights of intensity in the nineteenth century, and this fervor generally carried over into the start of World War I.

In its depiction of the horror of war, *All Quiet on the Western Front* presents a scathing critique of the idea of nationalism, showing it to be a hollow, hypocritical ideology, a tool used by those in power to control a nation's populace. Paul and his friends are seduced into joining the army by nationalist ideas, but the experience of fighting quickly schools them in nationalism's irrelevance in the face of the war's horrors. The relative worthlessness on the battlefield of the patriots Kantorek and Himmelstoss accentuates the inappropriateness of outmoded ideals in modern warfare. Remarque illustrates that soldiers on the front fight not for the glory of their nation but rather for their own survival; they kill to keep from being killed. Additionally, Paul and his friends do not consider the opposing armies to be their real enemies; in their view, their real enemies are the men in power in their own nation, who they believe have sacrificed them to the war simply to increase their own power and glory.

Motifs

Motifs are recurring structures, contrasts, and literary devices that can help to develop and inform the text's major themes.

The Pressure of Patriotic Idealism

Many of the novel's harshest critiques of nationalism are reserved for the character of Kantorek, the teacher whose impassioned speeches convinced Paul and his friends to join the army at the onset of the war. Kantorek uses an idealistic, patriotic, and poetic rhetoric to convey the concepts of national loyalty and glory. In his letter to the young men, for instance, he calls them "Iron Youth," implying that they are hard, strong, and resilient, a description that fails to consider the horror of the war, which traps the men in a constant state of panic and despair. As Kantorek and his speeches are recalled throughout the novel, Paul and his friends become increasingly disgusted by them; their experience of war has made them increasingly cynical about patriotism and nationalism. Even at the start of the novel, they blame Kantorek for Joseph Behm's untimely death, claiming that the teacher failed to understand that no lofty ideal can possibly offer physical or emotional protection or comfort in the heat of battle.

Carnage and Gore

The novel's main weapon against patriotic idealism is simply its unrelenting portrayal of the carnage and gore that the war occasions. Every battle scene (roughly every other chapter) features brutal violence and bloody descriptions of death and injury. Hospital scenes portray men with grisly wounds that go untreated because of insufficient medical supplies. Paul carries the wounded Kat on his back to safety, only to discover that Kat's head was hit by a piece of shrapnel while Paul was carrying him. As part of the overall exploration of disconnection from one's feelings, death is treated with impersonal efficiency: the cook wonders whether regulations permit him to give the surviving soldiers the dead men's rations; when Kemmerich dies, he is hauled away with the tears still wet on his face so that another soldier can have his bed. Amid this horrific violence and numbness, the overblown phrases of nationalistic rhetoric quickly lose their persuasive power and take on a loathsome quality of hypocrisy and ignorance.

Animal Instinct

Remarque indicates throughout the novel that the only way for a soldier to survive battle is to turn off his mind and operate solely on instinct, becoming less like a human being and more like an animal. Paul thinks of himself as a "human animal," and the other soldiers who survive multiple battles operate in the same way. The experience of battle is quite animalistic in this way, as the soldiers trust their senses over their thoughts and sniff out safety wherever they can find it. This motif of animal instinct contributes to the larger theme that war destroys the humanity of the soldier, stripping away his ability to feel and, in this case, making him act like a beast rather than a man.

Symbols

Symbols are objects, characters, figures, and colors used to represent abstract ideas or concepts.

Kemmerich's Boots

All Quiet on the Western Front doesn't employ a great deal of symbolism, but one important symbol in the novel is Kemmerich's boots. Kemmerich's high, supple boots are passed from soldier to soldier as each owner dies in sequence. Kemmerich himself took them from the corpse of a dead airman, and as Kemmerich lies on his own deathbed, Müller immediately begins maneuvering to receive the boots. Paul brings them to Müller after Kemmerich dies and inherits them himself when Müller is shot to death later in the novel. In this way, the boots represent the cheapness of human life in the war. A good pair of boots is more valuable—and more durable—than a human life. The question of who will inherit them continually overshadows their owners' deaths. The boots also symbolize the necessary pragmatism that a soldier must have. One cannot yield to one's emotions amid the devastation of the war; rather, one must block out grief and despair like a machine.

Summary & Analysis

Chapter One

> *It will try simply to tell of a generation of men who, even though they may have escaped shells, were destroyed by the war.*
>
> *(See* QUOTATIONS, *p. 51)*

Summary

This statement, from the novel's epigraph, sets up the intent of *All Quiet on the Western Front*: to discuss a generation of men who, though they survived the war physically, were destroyed by it mentally.

Chapter One opens with Paul Bäumer, the narrator, and the other members of the Second Company, a unit of German soldiers fighting during World War I, resting after being relieved from the front lines. They have spent the last two weeks at the front in constant battle. Out of a company originally comprised of 150 men, only eighty returned after a heavy attack on the last day.

Paul describes his fellow soldiers: he, Leer, Müller, and Kropp are all nineteen years old. They are from the same class in school, and each enlisted in the army voluntarily. Tjaden, a locksmith, is a voracious eater but remains thin as a rail, making Paul wonder where all the food goes to on his skinny frame. Haie Westhus, also nineteen, is a peat-digger with a body as large and powerful as Tjaden's is thin. Detering is a peasant with a wife at home. Katczinsky, the unofficial leader of Paul's small group of comrades, is a cunning older man of about forty years.

After a sound night's sleep, the men line up for breakfast. The cook has unwittingly made enough food for 150 men. The men are anxious to eat the rations designated for their fallen comrades, but the cook insists that he is only allowed to distribute single rations and that the dead soldiers' rations will simply have to go to waste. After a heated argument, however, he agrees to distribute all of the food.

Paul remembers that he and his friends were embarrassed to use the general latrines when they were recruits. Now they find them a luxury. Every soldier is intimately acquainted with his stomach and intestines. The men settle down to rest, smoke, and play cards in order to forget about their narrow survival during their last trip to the front. Kemmerich, one of Paul's classmates and a member of the Second Company, is in the hospital with a thigh wound.

Paul recalls his schoolmaster, Kantorek, a fiercely patriotic man who persuaded many of Paul's friends to enlist as volunteers to prove their patriotism. Joseph Behm, one such young man, was hesitant but eventually gave in to Kantorek's unrelenting pressure. He was one of the first to die, and his death was particularly horrible. With Behm's death, Paul and his classmates lost their innocent trust in authority figures such as Kantorek. Kantorek writes a letter to them filled with the empty phrases of patriotic fervor, calling them "Iron Youth" and glorifying their heroism. The men reflect that they once idolized Kantorek but now despise him; they blame him for pushing them into the army and exposing them to the horror of war.

The men go to see Kemmerich, who is unaware that his leg has been amputated. Paul discerns from his sallow skin that Kemmerich will not live long. The men give some cigarettes to an orderly in return for his agreement to give Kemmerich a dose of morphine to ease his pain. Müller, reasoning that a one-legged man has no need for matching shoes, wants Kemmerich's boots for himself, but Paul discourages him from pressing the matter further. They will have to keep watch until Kemmerich dies and then take the boots before the orderlies steal them.

> *The first bombardment showed us our mistake, and under it the world as they had taught it to us broke in pieces.*
>
> *(See* QUOTATIONS, *p. 52)*

ANALYSIS

The opening chapter of *All Quiet on the Western Front* is devoted to presenting the novel's main themes: the horror of war and its effect on the ordinary soldier. Earlier novels about war and soldiers tended to emphasize heroism, romance, and glory on the battlefield, leaving out the terror and dehumanizing violence of military conflict. Like Stephen Crane's *The Red Badge of Courage, All Quiet on the Western Front* presents the gruesome specter of war as it actually exists and as soldiers experience it.

Everything about the first chapter of *All Quiet on the Western Front* conveys to the reader that this is a new sort of war novel. Its newness was in many ways appropriate, because World War I was also a new sort of war. Before World War I, wars generally did not involve nonstop fighting over a period of years. Often, the armies were comprised of hired mercenaries, professionals who fought seasonally. The opening of the novel paints a very different picture: Remarque's soldiers are volunteers or conscripts. For Paul and his classmates, the army has become an expression of patriotic duty; they do not perceive it as a career. Outside the classroom, young men of their age faced ostracism and condemnation from society if they did not join the war effort as volunteers. In England, able-bodied men of the same age faced similar pressure to join the army.

World War I exploded out of nationalism, a political ideology that swept Europe during the nineteenth century. Under this ideology, the citizen was expected to give unquestioning loyalty to the state. These romantic ideals of the nineteenth century were at odds with the reality of modern trench warfare. Paul and his classmates are caught in this disjuncture between the idealism of the Great War, represented by Kantorek's impassioned rhetoric, and its reality of blood and death, represented by the death of Joseph Behm and the impending death of Kemmerich.

The first chapter emphasizes, at every turn, the unheroic, unglamorous, horrifying life of a soldier in World War I, underscoring the extent to which the brutalities of war strip away the moral and mannered aspects of human beings. The horrors of war have become so routine that Paul mentions that nearly half of his company was killed with the same detachment that marks his descriptions of mundane details. The other characters share this desensitization. The cook's main concern is not that seventy men have been injured or killed but whether he should dole out the rations for a full company to the remaining survivors. These survivors, likewise, are more concerned with whether they will receive enough to eat than with the deaths of their friends and comrades. This shockingly callous attitude serves the structural function of creating suspense and motivating development of the story—one wonders what could have scarred Paul and his friends to make them behave in such a way.

Kantorek's letter is particularly disgusting to Paul and his friends because of what it reveals about the older generation's attitude toward the younger men who fight in the war. In calling Paul and his friends "Iron Youth," Kantorek implies that they are young, impassive, and strong. But Paul and his friends do not feel impassive; rather, they feel as though they are losing their minds.

Nor do they feel young—the hell of combat has aged them beyond their years. Paul and his friends feel that older men such as Kantorek have betrayed their trust and sent them to die for empty and useless ideals.

Chapter Two

Summary

Paul recalls his life before the war. As a young student, he used to write poetry. Now, he feels empty and cynical, thinking that his short time as a soldier has taught him more hard lessons about life than a decade at school could. He has no interest in, or time for, poetry, and his parents now seem to him a hazy and unreliable memory. He feels that "only facts are real and important to us."

Paul ruminates that he and the other young men of his generation were cut off from life just as they had begun to live it. The older soldiers have jobs and families to which they can return after the war, but the younger men have nothing; the war has become their entire lives. Whereas the older men will forget the trenches and the death, the young men have nothing definite on which to focus thoughts of the future. Their prewar lives are vague, unreal dreams with no relevance to the world that has been created by the war. Paul feels utterly cut off from humanity; his only feelings of love and loyalty are those that he shares with his friends and fellow soldiers. As a result, Paul tries to see them in the best possible light. He thinks about Müller's attempt to persuade the dying Kemmerich to give him his boots and tries to convince himself that Müller was being reasonable rather than inconsiderate.

During training, Paul and his classmates were taught that patriotism requires suppressing individuality and personality, a sacrifice that civilians do not require of even the lowest class of servants. Corporal Himmelstoss, formerly a postman, trained Paul's platoon. He was a small, petty man who relentlessly humiliated his recruits, especially Paul, Tjaden, Haie, and Kropp. Eventually, Paul and the others learned to stand up to Himmelstoss's authority without outright defiance. Paul and his friends detested Himmelstoss, but now Paul knows that the humiliation and the arbitrary discipline toughened them and probably helped them to survive as long as they have. He believes that had Himmelstoss not hardened the men, their experiences on the front lines would have driven them insane.

Kemmerich is very near death. He is saddened by the fact that he will never become a head forester, as he had hoped. Paul attends Kemmerich's death throes. He lies next to his friend to try to comfort him, assuring him that he will get well and return home. Kemmerich knows that his leg is gone, and Paul tries to cheer him with talk about the advances in the construction of artificial limbs. Kemmerich tells Paul to give his boots to Müller. Kemmerich begins to cry silently and refuses to respond to Paul's attempts at conversation. Paul goes to find the doctor, who refuses to come. When Paul returns to Kemmerich's bedside, Kemmerich is already dead. His body is immediately taken from the bed to clear room for another wounded soldier. Paul takes Kemmerich's boots to Müller.

Analysis

Whereas the first chapter focused on the soldiers' external experience, emphasizing the physical repulsiveness, horrific violence, and exhaustion of war, the second chapter focuses on Paul's inner state, exploring the toll taken by the war on the humanity of an individual soldier. Though Paul feels cynical, lonely, and empty, Remarque highlights his good qualities: Paul is at heart an intelligent, kindhearted, sensitive young man. The brutality of World War I has damaged his psyche, and the only way for him to survive is to shut himself off from his feelings, accepting a numbness that he experiences as cynicism and despair.

This process of cutting oneself off from one's own feelings in order to endure the hardship of war is repeated throughout the novel and is shown to be the primary method by which war strips one of one's humanity. In this chapter, for instance, the doctor refuses to see Kemmerich because he has already amputated five legs that day; he can tolerate no more, and he simply shuts himself off from his feelings of sympathy and compassion, allowing Kemmerich to die in pain rather than expose himself to any more tragedy and gore. It is impossible to blame the doctor in this situation; Remarque emphasizes that war forces everyone, including doctors, to confront more than they can possibly stomach. The horror of war is that one must cut oneself off in this way simply to endure it. One's own feelings become as dangerous an enemy as the opposing army.

Kemmerich's death extends the criticism of romantic illusions about the war. He dies from a relatively light wound that probably became infected—there is no glory in his death. Here Kantorek's patriotic exhortations fail. In modern warfare, there is no room for refined notions of honor, nor for sentimentality. Müller needs Kemmerich's boots; it is not that he or any of the other survivors are not affected by their friend's death but rather that they cannot allow themselves to dwell on their grief. In this way, the boots become one of the novel's most important symbols of the cheapness of life: the boots repeatedly outlive their owners, and each time the man wearing them dies, the question of who will inherit the boots overshadows the death. Life on the front is dangerous, ugly, dirty, and miserable; the soldiers do not have adequate food and clothing, and so the day-to-day matters of survival take precedence over sentimentality. The men cannot afford to act otherwise; dwelling on each friend's death would lead to madness.

Chapter Three

Summary

A group of new recruits arrives to reinforce the decimated company, making Paul and his friends feel like grizzled veterans. More than twenty of the reinforcements for the Second Company are only about seventeen years old. Kat gives one of the new recruits some beans that he acquired by bribing the company's cook. He warns the boy to bring tobacco next time as payment for the food. Kat's ability to scrounge extra food and provisions amazes Paul. Kat is a cobbler by trade, but he has an uncanny knack for making the most of life on the front.

Kat believes that if every soldier got the same food and the same pay, the war would end quickly. Kropp proposes that the declaration of wars should be conducted like a festival. He thinks that the generals and national leaders should battle one another with clubs in an open arena—the country with the last survivor wins the war.

Paul and his friends remember the recruits' barracks with longing now. Even Himmelstoss's petty humiliations seem idyllic in comparison to the actual war. They muse that Himmelstoss must have been different as a postman and wonder why he is such a bully as a drill sergeant. Kropp mimics Himmelstoss and shouts, "Change at Löhne," recalling a drill in which Himmelstoss forced them to practice changing trains at a railway station. Kat suggests that Himmelstoss is like a lot of other men. He remarks that even a dog trained to eat potatoes will snap at meat given the opportunity. Men behave the same way when given the opportunity to have a little authority. Every man is a beast underneath all his manners and customs.

The army is based on one man having more power over another man. Kat believes the problem is that they have too much power. Civilians are not permitted to torment others the way men in the army torment one another. Tjaden arrives and excitedly reports that Himmelstoss is coming to the front. Paul explains that Tjaden holds a grudge against Himmelstoss. Tjaden is a bed wetter, and during training, Himmelstoss set out to break him of this habit, which he attributed to laziness. He found another bed wetter, Kindervater, and forced them to sleep in the same set of bunk beds. Every night, they traded places. The one on the bottom was drenched by the other's urine during the night. The problem was not laziness but bad health, rendering Himmelstoss's ploy ineffective. The man assigned to the bottom often slept on the floor and thus caught a cold.

Haie, Paul, Kropp, and Tjaden plotted their revenge upon Himmelstoss. They lay in wait for him one night on a dark road as he returned from his favorite pub. When he approached, they threw a bed cover over his head, and Haie punched him senseless. They stripped him of his pants and took turns lashing him with a whip, muffling his shouts with a pillow. They slipped away, and Himmelstoss never discovered who gave him the beating.

Analysis

After sketching the common soldier's experience in Chapters One and Two, Remarque offers more detailed character portraits in Chapter Three. This imbuing of characters with individual personalities is essential to the thematic concerns of the novel. *All Quiet on the Western Front* indicts not only the horrors of combat but also the dehumanizing impersonality that attends the entire machinery of war; for this indictment to be successful, the text must show how distinct, human personas are chewed up by a machine that treats them only as able bodies. Although Kemmerich's death in Chapter One is sad, the reader never really meets Kemmerich; the scene reveals more about his friends than it does about him. The introduction of more fully drawn characters such as Kat, in Chapter Three, enables Remarque to render their eventual pointless dehumanization and death as truly tragic. Of course, the presence of individualized characters hardly makes this text unique, but one should bear in mind that these characters constantly confront a system that denies them any individuality and that this tension animates much of the novel. The mindless drilling, such as the "Change at Löhne" exercise and Himmelstoss's stupid and cruel solution to Tjaden's bed-wetting, expose an impersonal, highly rationalized military that does not serve even its own interests: the "Change at Löhne" drill is a waste of time, and Himmelstoss's solution only makes matters worse.

Paul's description of Kat introduces a response to dehumanized conditions and, with it, a transfigured concept of the hero. Kat, like traditional heroes, is a natural leader and adept at many trades. His interest, though, is in lessening his own suffering and that of his friends, not in self-sacrifice or bravery. His enemy is modern warfare, not the English or the French. Moreover, his struggle against modern warfare has a historical dimension: Remarque associates Kat with the artifacts and behavior of premodern society. He is a cobbler by trade, an old-fashioned, preindustrial livelihood. When Kat and his friends have to sleep on uncomfortable metal wire inside a factory, a markedly modern scenario, Kat finds a horse-box with straw, which they use to pad their beds. But what truly distinguishes Kat as a walking anachronism is the freedom and self-reliance with which he moves through army life. The ingenuity and confidence that allow him to find boxes of lobsters are what marked, in epic war stories, the hero on the battlefield. For Remarque, this type of hero no longer exists, but Kat's ability to think and act for himself survives in his resistance to dehumanized conditions.

Kat's rant about the brutal hierarchies of the military blames the suffering that soldiers endure on a fundamental human sadism. Though Paul and Kropp volunteer theories about why officers are needlessly cruel, the text privileges Kat's opinions by letting Kat air them to a greater extent than others are allowed to air their opinions, and by having the others defer to him in the end. Kat argues that officers are cruel to those ranked below them because they enjoy exercising power that they do not have in civilian life; a certain company commander's "head has been turned by having so much power." This sadism is a kind of class warfare. Kat maintains that the lower one's station in civil society, the more power corrupts one in the army.

Remarque complicates Kat's complaints, however, with the account of the beating of Himmelstoss, which went beyond a mere prank; it was brutal, as Himmelstoss was whipped and partially suffocated. Haie, whose name means "sharks" in German, bent over Himmelstoss "with a fiendish grin and his mouth open with bloodlust." Paul describes him winding up "as if he were going to reach down a star," an ironic play on Himmelstoss's name, which consists

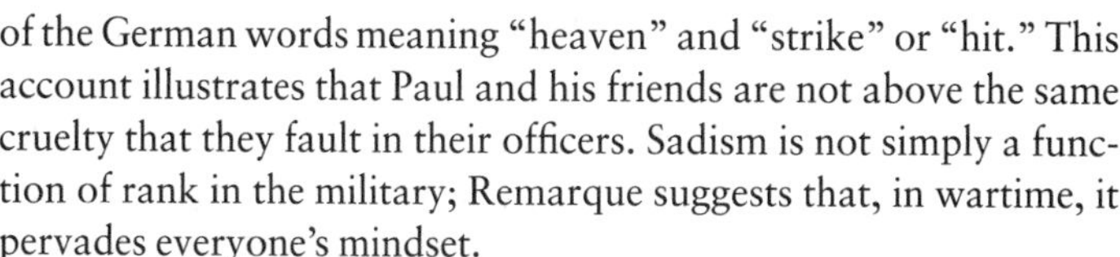

of the German words meaning "heaven" and "strike" or "hit." This account illustrates that Paul and his friends are not above the same cruelty that they fault in their officers. Sadism is not simply a function of rank in the military; Remarque suggests that, in wartime, it pervades everyone's mindset.

Chapter Four

> *We march up, moody or good-tempered soldiers—we reach the zone where the front begins and become on the instant human animals.*
>
> *(See* QUOTATIONS, *p. 53)*

Summary

The Second Company is assigned to lay barbed wire at the front, an extremely dangerous task. As the men's trucks rumble toward the front, they pass a house, and Paul hears the cackle of geese. He and Kat agree to come back later, take the geese, and feast on them. The sound of gunfire and shells fills the air, gripping the new recruits with fear. Kat explains to the recruits how to distinguish which guns are firing by listening to the blasts. He announces that he senses there will be a bombardment later in the night: the English batteries have begun firing an hour earlier than usual. Paul reflects that the roar of guns and whistling of shells sharpens men's senses.

Paul ruminates that, for the soldier, the earth takes on a new significance at the front: he buries his body in it for shelter, and it receives him every time he throws himself down in a fold, furrow, or hollow. At the front, a man's ancient animal instincts awaken. They are a saving grace for many men who obey them without hesitation. Often, a man drops to the ground just in time to avoid a shell that he did not even hear coming. On the front, men are transformed from soldiers into "human animals."

The soldiers carry wire and iron rods to the front. After they lay the wire, they try to sleep until the trucks arrive to drive them back. Kat's prediction that they would be bombarded is correct. Everyone scrambles for cover while the shells land around them. Paul attempts to place a terrified recruit's helmet back on the recruit's head, but the boy cowers under Paul's arm. Paul places the helmet on the recruit's behind to protect it from shell fragments. After the shelling lessens, the recruit comes to and notices with embarrassment that he has defecated in his pants. Paul explains that many soldiers experience this problem at first. He instructs the boy to remove his underpants and throw them away.

The men hear the wrenching sounds of wounded horses shrieking in agony. Detering is particularly horrified because he is a farmer and loves horses. After the wounded men are gathered, those in charge of shooting the wounded animals do their job. Detering declares with disgust that using horses in war is the "vilest baseness."

As the trucks drive the men back, Kat becomes restless. A flurry of bombs then lands around them. The men take cover in a nearby graveyard. Paul crawls under an uncovered coffin for protection. Kat shakes him from behind to tell him to put his gas mask on. After he dons his mask, Paul helps a new recruit put his on. He then dives into a hole created by an exploding shell, reasoning that shells seldom hit the same place twice. Kat and Kropp join him. Paul takes a breath on the valve of the mask, hoping that the mask is airtight.

Later, Paul climbs out and sees a soldier not wearing his mask who appears to be okay. Paul tears his mask off and gulps fresh air. The shelling has stopped. Paul notices a recruit lying on the ground with his hip a mess of flesh and bone splinters at the joint. It is the recruit who defecated in his pants earlier. Kat and Paul know that he will not survive his wounds. Kat whispers that it would be merciful of them to end his life with a gunshot before the agony of his wound begins to torment him. Before they can end the recruit's life, however, other soldiers begin to emerge from their holes.

Analysis

Remarque uses the men's lorry ride to bring the reader to the front. The description of the bombardment is one of the most poetic and dramatic parts of the novel, and it requires a certain preparation. During the lorry ride, Remarque builds suspense with terse, opaque sentences: "We have to go on wiring fatigue. The motor lorries roll up. We climb in." The necessity implied by "have to" resonates in the narrator's refusal to embellish these mute facts. In a style similar to that of his contemporary and fellow war novelist Ernest Hemingway, Remarque excises adjectives and adverbs and leaves only nouns and verbs that exist and move of their accord, above human intervention. The reportage style of phrases such as "The engines drone, the lorries bump and rattle" makes Paul's powerlessness and resignation evident. Events hit and pass through him to the reader like bullets on a predetermined course.

Paul's description of the soldier's relationship with the earth is full of sexual metaphors and imagery and alludes to the relationship between mother and child. The sexual imagery of "folds, and hollows, and holes" and men thrusting iron rods into the earth combined with the idea of the earth as mother suggest an Oedipal relationship between the soldier and earth. (The Oedipal Complex, which involves sexual desire for one's parent of the opposite sex, is a psychoanalytical concept posited by Sigmund Freud. The title refers to Oedipus, who, in Sophocles' *Oedipus the King,* unknowingly kills his father and marries his mother.)

Although this Freudian interpretation is complicated by the fact that the earth is almost everything to the soldier—brother, friend, and mother—the sexual and maternal systems of imagery predominate, and the assessment of Oedipal desire proves consistent with other kinds of regression and reversal described in the chapter. Paul declares that soldiers must become like animals in order to survive; the fact that Detering attributes to animals some degree of human dignity in war completes this reversal. A veteran accustomed to human suffering, Detering cannot bear to hear horses cry in agony. He feels that they are more blameless for the war than a private in the trenches, who, by being human, somehow shares responsibility for the war. "I'd like to know what harm they've done," he asks. The graveyard scene blurs the boundaries between the living and the dead: Paul wonders for a moment, half-seriously, whether a dead man has awakened and grabbed him. He survives the shelling by burrowing under a coffin; indeed, the war has left him, in a sense, more dead than the corpse disinterred by the bombardment.

Paul's reaction to the front strips the romanticism out of the war experience. He does not speak of the honor and glory of fighting for one's country; rather, he comments that the soldier fights for his life. He relies on instinct to save himself from bullets and bombs and concentrates on acquiring food, clothing, and shelter rather than on an abstract ideal of patriotic duty to the fatherland. He must learn to cope with constant fear, uncertainty, bombardment, and violence by regressing from his human sensitivities into a state of animalistic and instinctive self-preservation.

Chapter Five

Summary

Paul describes the unsanitary conditions of life at the front. Tjaden, tired of killing lice one by one, scrapes them off his skin into a boot-polish tin. He kills them by heating the tin with a flame. Haie's lice have red crosses on their heads, and he jokes that he got them at a hospital where they attended the surgeon general.

Himmelstoss has arrived in the camp, proving the rumor true. He was caught tormenting his recruits excessively and has been sent to the front as punishment. Müller begins asking everyone what they would do if the war ended suddenly. Kropp says the war will not end, but Müller persists. Kat mentions his wife and children. The younger men mention women and getting drunk. Haie says that he would become a noncommissioned army officer since digging peat, his old job, is such a terrible occupation. Tjaden states that he would concentrate on getting revenge on Himmelstoss. Detering says that he would return to his farm.

Himmelstoss approaches the men, who rudely ignore him. He orders Tjaden to stand, but Tjaden moons him in response. Tjaden rushes off to hide before Himmelstoss returns with the authorities. Müller continues with his questions. They calculate that there are only twelve men left out of the twenty from their class who joined the army. Seven are dead, four are wounded, and one went insane. They mockingly recite questions that Kantorek shot at them in school. Paul cannot imagine what he will do after the war. Kropp concludes that the war has destroyed everything for them. They are not impetuous youths anymore but men perpetually on the run. They cannot believe in anything except the war.

Himmelstoss returns with the sergeant-major to punish Tjaden. Paul and the others refuse to tell him where Tjaden is hiding. The sergeant-major solves the problem by declaring that Tjaden must report to the Orderly Room within ten minutes. The men resolve to torment Himmelstoss at every opportunity. Himmelstoss returns later to demand that they tell him where Tjaden is. Kropp insults him, and Himmelstoss storms off.

Later that evening, Kropp and Tjaden are put on trial for insubordination. Paul and the others tell the court about Himmelstoss's cruelty toward Tjaden during training. After hearing their story, the presiding lieutenant gives Tjaden and Kropp light punishments and lectures Himmelstoss about his behavior. Tjaden receives three days open arrest and Kropp receives one. Paul and the others visit them in the makeshift jail and play cards.

Kat and Paul bribe a driver of a munitions wagon with two cigarettes to take them back to the house where they heard the geese. Paul climbs over the fence and enters the shed to find two geese. He grabs both and slams their heads against the wall, hoping to avoid a commotion. The attempt fails, and the geese cackle and fight with him furiously before he manages to escape with one goose in hand. Kat kills it quickly, and they retreat to an unused lean-to to cook it, eating quickly for fear of their theft being discovered. They keep the feathers to make pillows. Paul feels an intimate closeness with Kat as they roast the goose. They eat their fill and take the rest to Tjaden and Kropp.

Analysis

Müller's persistent questioning about his friends' postwar plans reveals why the young generation of men who enlisted right out of school was termed "the lost generation" by Gertrude Stein, an American writer who spent much of her life in Paris. Older men who had prewar jobs and families regarded the war as an interruption in their lives that eventually would end. They had concrete identities and functions within society. Younger men, such as Paul and his classmates, had no such concrete identities. They entered the war when they were on the threshold of their adult lives. None of them have definite answers to Müller's questions: they no longer have any conception of themselves apart from the war, emphasizing the theme of the war's ravaging effect on the humanity of soldiers.

Remarque's soldiers, like many members of the lost generation, regard the war as something that could not possibly end because they cannot imagine anything else. They thus conceive their adult identities as inextricably linked to their lives as soldiers. Haie gives the most definite postwar plans, but even his answer involves remaining in the army—he cannot imagine himself as anything but a soldier. Paul and his younger comrades cannot imagine functioning in civilian jobs after what they have seen and done. Their only definite plan for the future is to exact revenge upon Himmelstoss. Their curt answers to Müller's questions betray a certain anxiety about the end of the war, as if they fear the end of the war as much as they fear the war itself. Thinking and planning for the future requires concrete forms of hope, but the horror of trench warfare doesn't allow them to have hope for anything other than survival. They have no experiences as adults that do not involve a day-to-day struggle to survive and maintain sanity.

Although he is not particularly important to the novel's narrative, Himmelstoss, like Kantorek, is a very significant figure in *All Quiet on the Western Front* because of what he reveals about the mentality of war. Paul and his friends observe repeatedly that war makes small, petty men become arrogant and hungry for power. Himmelstoss is the perfect example, a former mailman who becomes a fearsome bully simply because he is given military authority. Paul continually differentiates between the ceremonial, formal aspects of the army and the hellish chaos of actual battle. He sees little relation between parade drilling and saluting, on the one hand, and the madness of combat, on the other. Until he arrives at the front, Himmelstoss represents only the useless formal rituals of the army, demanding that men salute him on sight. Paul's friends observe that the German army is losing the war because the soldiers know how to salute too well, implying that too much attention is paid to outmoded propriety and not enough to the actual techniques of fighting in a modern war.

Paul and his friends continue to form an extremely close-knit unit in this chapter. The novel simultaneously explores the horror of war and the intensity of soldiers' friendships. Remarque suggests that peacetime social relationships can never approach the intimacy or intensity of a soldier's bonds with other soldiers. Paul marvels at the flood of emotion that he experiences while roasting the stolen goose with Kat. He and Kat would never have known one another in peacetime, but the war has brought their lives together in a crucible of horror. Their shared suffering makes peacetime concerns and concepts of friendship pale by comparison. In many ways, the bond forged between soldiers in trench warfare is the only romanticized element of Remarque's spectacularly unromantic novel.

Chapter Six

Summary

The Second Company returns to the front two days early. On their way, they pass a schoolhouse that has been shattered by shells. Fresh coffins are piled by the dozens already lying next to the schoolhouse. The soldiers make jokes to distance themselves from the unpleasant knowledge that the coffins have been made for them. At the front, they listen to the enemy transports and guns.

They detect that the enemy is bringing troops to the front, and they can hear that the English have strengthened their artillery. The men are disheartened by this knowledge as well as by the fact that their own shells are beginning to fall in their trenches—the barrels on the guns are worn out.

The soldiers can do nothing but wait. Chance determines whether things will take a turn for the better or for the worse. Paul relates that he once left a dugout to visit friends in a different dugout. When he returned to the first, it had been completely demolished by a direct hit. He returned to the second only to discover that it had been buried.

The soldiers have to fight the fat, aggressive rats to protect their food. Large rations of cheese and rum are doled out to the men, and every man receives numerous grenades and ample ammunition. The men remove saw blades from their bayonets because the enemy instantly kills anyone caught with this kind of blade on his bayonet. Kat is in bad spirits, which Paul takes as a bad sign, since Kat has an uncanny sense for knowing what will happen on the front.

Days pass before the bombs begin to fall. No attack comes right away, but the bombing continues. Attempts to deliver food to the dugouts fail. Even Kat fails to scrounge anything up. The men settle down to wait. Eventually, a new recruit cracks and attempts to leave. Kat and Paul have to beat him into submission. Later, the dugout suffers a direct hit. Luckily, the shell is a light one, and the concrete holds up against it. Three recruits crack, and one actually escapes the dugout. Before Paul can retrieve him, a shell whistles through the air and smashes the escaped recruit to bits. They have to bind another recruit to subdue him. Everyone else tries to play cards, but no one can concentrate on the game.

Finally, the shelling lessens. The attack has come. Paul and his comrades throw grenades out of the dugout before jumping out. The French attackers suffer heavy losses from the German machine guns and grenades. The soldiers kill with a mindless fury after days of waiting helplessly in the dark while the bombs fell above them. The Germans repel the attack and reach the enemy lines. They wreak havoc and destruction before grabbing all of the provisions they can carry. They run back to their position to rest for an hour. They devour the tins of food they have gathered, noting that the enemy has far better provisions than they do.

Later, Paul stands watch. Memories of the past come to him. The calm and quiet memories bring sorrow rather than desire. He muses that desires "belong to another world that is gone from us." He is sure that his youth is lost and that he has become permanently numb and indifferent.

Days pass while dead men accumulate on both sides. Paul and his comrades listen to one man's death throes for three days. They are unable to locate him despite their best efforts. The new recruits figure heavily in the dead and wounded; these reinforcements have had little training, and they drop like flies on the front.

During an attack, Paul finds Himmelstoss in a dugout, pretending to be wounded. Paul tries to force him out with blows and threats, but Himmelstoss does not give in until a nearby lieutenant orders both of them to proceed. They rush forward with the attack. The old hands try to teach some of the new recruits combat tricks and wisdom during the hours of rest, but the recruits do everything wrong when the fighting begins again. Haie receives a fatal wound. When the Second Company is relieved, only thirty-two of the original 150 men remain.

Analysis

In this gruesome chapter, Remarque fuses together all of the preceding focuses of the novel—physical repulsiveness and gore, psychological drain, the animalistic savagery of battle—as the bombardment wreaks havoc on the men in the trenches. With its in-depth look at the grim reality of trench warfare, this chapter deals with some of the most hideous historical details of combat in World War I.

Before modern trench warfare, inventive military strategies and sweeping victories were possible. As the endless, grinding attack in this chapter illustrates, World War I quickly became characterized by battles of attrition. The goal was not "victory" but rather the wearing down of the enemy's ability to attack or even continue the war. The strategy was simple: the attacking side bombarded enemy trenches relentlessly, sometimes for up to a week. The death toll from bombardment compared to the death toll in the actual attack was comparatively low. The Germans in particular built strong bomb-proof dugouts, although those built later were of lesser quality. After the bombardment, a wave of attacking soldiers advanced on the enemy trenches.

Unfortunately, as we see in this chapter, the defending side knew that the attack was coming the moment the bombing ended. The result was an ever-growing collection of bodies in No Man's Land, the space between the trenches that neither army controlled. The major battles of attrition in World War I resulted in hundreds of thousands of casualties, making them among the bloodiest battles in human history. There really was no "victor" because the gains usually constituted a few hundred yards of ground. Generally, they ended in stalemate, with an unprecedented cost in human lives and human suffering.

Paul's description of the German response to the attack leaves no doubt as to the decidedly unromantic nature of trench warfare. Sensing the imminent French attack wave, Paul and his comrades are able to man their machine guns and mow down the attacking soldiers. However, they do not achieve this success out of patriotic fervor or bravery; indeed, they have removed the blades from their bayonets, thus making their weapons less effective, because they fear death more than they long to kill the enemy. They are not seekers of glory but rather men driven to the brink of insanity. They savagely kill and maim the attackers not because they are enemies of the fatherland but because they can do nothing else to release the anxiety, stress, and terror of a days-long bombardment.

Despite the success of the German soldiers' defense, this chapter provides numerous clues that Germany is losing the war. The English and the French have increased the strength of their artillery, while the German weapons are so badly worn that the German shells often fall into their own trenches, killing German soldiers. The new recruits are younger than ever before, and they have had scant training. As a result, they perish in numbers five to ten times greater than experienced soldiers do. In essence, it is clear that Germany is running out of able-bodied adult men: soldiers are being killed and wounded at such a debilitating rate that the German army cannot even effectively train the boys they send to replace the men they have lost.

Chapter Seven

> *We want to live at any price; so we cannot burden ourselves with feelings which . . . would be out of place here.*
>
> *(See* QUOTATIONS, *p. 54)*

Summary

The Second Company is sent to a depot for reorganization. Himmelstoss tries to make amends with the men after having experienced the horror of the front. He becomes generous with food and gets easy jobs for them; he even wins Tjaden over to his side. Good food and rest are enough to make a soldier content. Away from the trenches, Paul and his comrades make vulgar jokes as usual. Over time, their humorous jests become more bitter.

Paul, Leer, and Kropp meet three women while they are swimming. They communicate with them in broken French, indicating that they have food. They are forbidden to cross the canal, just as the women are. Later that night, the men gather some food and swim across, wearing nothing more than their boots. The women throw them clothing. Despite the language barrier, they chatter endlessly. They call the soldiers "poor boys." Paul is inexperienced, but he yields to desire. He hopes to recapture a piece of his innocence and youth with a woman who does not belong to the army brothels.

Paul receives seventeen days of leave. Afterward, he has to report to a training base, and will return to the front in six weeks. He wonders how many of his friends will survive six weeks. He visits one of the women on the other side of the canal, but she is not interested to hear about his leave. He realizes that she would find him more exciting if he were going to the front.

When Paul reaches his hometown, he finds that his mother is ill with cancer and that the civilian population is slowly starving. He cannot shake a feeling of "strangeness"; he no longer feels at home in his family's house. His mother asks if it was "very bad out there." Paul lies to her. He has no words to describe his experiences—at least no words that she would understand.

A major becomes angry that Paul does not salute him in the street. As a punishment, he forces Paul to do a march in the street and salute smartly. Paul wishes to avoid further such incidents, so he begins wearing civilian clothing. Paul's father, unlike his mother, keeps asking him questions. He doesn't understand that it is dangerous for Paul to put his experiences into words. Others who don't ask questions take too much pride in their silence. Sometimes the screeching of the trams startles Paul because it sounds like shells. He sits in his bedroom with his books and pictures, trying to recapture his childhood feelings of youth and desire, but the memories are only shadows. His identity as a soldier is the only thing to which he can cling.

Paul learns from a fellow classmate, Mittelstaedt, now a training officer, that Kantorek has been conscripted into the war. When he met Kantorek, Mittelstaedt tells Paul, he flaunted his authority as a superior officer over their old schoolmaster. He bitterly reminded Kantorek that he coerced Joseph Behm into enlisting against the boy's wishes—Joseph would have been called within three months anyway, and Mittelstaedt believes that Joseph died three months sooner than he would have otherwise. Mittelstaedt arranged to be placed in charge of Kantorek's company and has taken every chance to humiliate him, miming Kantorek's old admonitions as a schoolmaster.

Paul's mother becomes sadder as the end of Paul's leave looms closer. Paul visits Kemmerich's mother to deliver the news of her son's death. She demands to know how he died. Paul lies to her by telling her that he died quickly with little pain and suffering.

Paul's mother sits with Paul in his bedroom the last night of his leave. He tries to pretend that he is asleep, but he notes that she is in great physical pain. He urges her to return to bed. He wishes that he could weep in her lap and die with her. He also wishes that he had never come home on leave because it only awakens pain for himself and his mother.

Analysis

Paul, Leer, and Kropp's liaison with the three French women is an important psychological event in the novel. Most of Paul's sexual experiences have occurred in the army brothels, depriving him of another part of his youth. Moreover, that he seeks refuge in the arms of the enemy—the women are French—is thematically appropriate. In a sense, his actions imply that the redemption he seeks cannot come from his leaders or his fellow Germans: they have pressured him into the horrific trenches and betrayed him; they offer him prostitutes in the army brothels and destroy his youthful innocence.

However, Paul's woman does not offer him understanding or recognition of the value of his humanity. His romantic idealizations again clash with the harsh reality of the war that the young French woman represents: for her, Paul is nothing more than a passing, perhaps titillating, sentimental fantasy. She finds him attractive because he is young and lives in constant mortal danger on the front, but she loses interest upon hearing about his imminent leave. If she were never to see him again because he were returning to the front, he would be more exciting for her. While she wants him to be an abstract symbol, he wants her to see him as a human being. Similarly, the people at home who approach Paul do so because they want to be seen serving, or talking to, a soldier; for them, he is the representation of their romantic, patriotic ideals.

Like Kantorek and Himmelstoss, pompous, ridiculous, and power-hungry men, the major who humiliates Paul in public is yet another petty authority figure. He is obsessed with the distinctions and formalities of rank. Paul's feelings of betrayal come to the surface: the authority figures that demanded he become a soldier and fight do not demonstrate any understanding or respect for him even after all of the sacrifices that he has made and the horror through which he has lived.

Paul's reluctance to discuss with civilians his experiences in the trenches is due, in part, to his continuing need to maintain emotional distance from these terrible experiences. Putting his combat experiences and his reactions to them into words threatens the mental reserves that he will need when he returns to the front. His reluctance stems also from his knowledge that those who have never seen the ravages of trench warfare cannot possibly understand it; truthfully describing them might raise the risk of being branded unpatriotic. Lastly, Paul is a compassionate young man, and he fears that the truth about the war will cause pain for his family members, who, in their own way, are suffering as well.

Paul's visit to Kemmerich's mother likewise jeopardizes his ability to distance himself emotionally from his traumatic experiences. He faces the pain of a grieving mother, which threatens to open the gates of his own grief. He lies to her about the circumstances of her son's death because he cannot deal with his own anguish at having watched a friend die so miserably. He swears to her that he is telling the truth on everything that he holds sacred, not only because he wants to escape but also because he no longer truly holds anything sacred.

Chapter Eight

Summary

Paul reports to the training camp. Next to the camp is a prison for captured Russian soldiers, who are reduced to picking through the German soldiers' garbage for food. Paul can hardly understand how they find anything in the garbage: food is so scarce that everything is eaten. When he looks at the Russian soldiers, Paul can scarcely believe that these men with "honest peasant faces" are the enemy. Nothing about them suggests that he is fundamentally different from them or that he should have any reason to want to kill them. Many of the Russians are slowly starving, and they are stricken with dysentery in large numbers. Their soft voices bring images of warm, cozy homes to Paul's mind. But most people simply ignore the prisoners' begging, and a few even kick them.

The spirit of brotherhood among the prisoners touches Paul deeply. They live in such miserable circumstances that there is no longer any reason for them to fight among themselves. Paul cannot relate to them as individual men because he knows nothing of their lives; he only sees the animal suffering in them. People he has never met, people in positions of influence and power, said the word that made these men his enemy. Because of other men, he and they are required to shoot, maim, imprison, and kill one another. Paul pushes these thoughts away because they threaten his ability to maintain his composure. He breaks all of his cigarettes in half and gives them to the prisoners. One of the prisoners learns that Paul plays the piano. The prisoner plays his violin next to the fence. The music sounds thin and lonely in the night air, and only makes Paul feel sadder.

Before Paul returns to the front, his sister and father visit him. Their time together is as uncomfortable as it had been at home during Paul's leave, and they cannot find anything to talk about except his mother's illness. The hours are an agony for them. Paul's mother has been taken to the hospital to be treated for her cancer. His father says that he did not even dare to ask the hospital what the operation would cost because he feared that the doctors would not perform the surgery if he did.

Before they leave, Paul's father and sister give Paul some jam and potato cakes that his mother made for him. Depressed, Paul has no appetite for them, and ponders whether to give them to the hungry Russian prisoners. He decides that he will, but then he remembers that his mother must have been in pain when she made the cakes and that she meant them for him. He compromises by giving the prisoners two of the cakes.

Analysis

Paul's experience with the Russian prisoners in this chapter is one of Remarque's most powerful attacks on the patriotic, nationalistic ideals of the war. During World War I, nationalistic spirit drove the armies of several countries into unprecedented levels of carnage. The leaders of the warring nations disseminated propaganda to their citizens declaring a fundamental difference between themselves and the enemy. When Paul sees the Russians, however, they do not appear to be part of an abstract force that threatens his fatherland. They seem simply to be suffering individuals, and Paul cannot see them as his enemies. They remind him of German peasants and seem no different and no less human. He realizes, however, that when these prisoners were free they were no doubt ordered to kill German soldiers like himself. Remarque implies that the shared experience of humanity is more basic and more morally relevant than the arbitrary classifications of nationalism.

While the rhetoric of politics makes no sense to Paul, the rhetoric of music does. Though he knows nothing specific about the Russian prisoners' lives, he understands the comradeship of suffering, something that he himself has experienced in the trenches. Aware that Paul, too, is a musician, the Russian prisoner attempts to communicate with him via a mutually comprehensible language of emotion. His plaintive violin music touches Paul—one of the few instances in which Paul displays emotion—reinforcing Remarque's proposition that there is something universal in human existence that outweighs all perceived differences between people.

In advancing this argument, this chapter again looks at the role of political power in initiating military conflict and concludes that the powerful people who decide to wage war are the common soldier's real enemies. Paul reflects that he and the Russian prisoners are supposed to be enemies simply because other people more powerful than he and the prisoners decreed it so, not because of anything intrinsic to Paul, the Russians, or their relationship. Someone else decided that they had to shoot, kill, and torture one another, denying one another's humanity and finally destroying their own.

Before he takes this thought too far, Paul quickly flees it, driven again by the necessity of keeping himself detached from the full force of his feelings. He knows that if he thinks too deeply about the causes of participation in the war, his thoughts will only make the senselessness of everything that he has experienced all too apparent. The idea of acknowledging that the war is meaningless threatens Paul's last reserve of hope. He decides to save his thoughts for a later time because he cannot afford the psychological damage that they would cause him now.

Paul's interaction with his father and sister in this chapter further illustrates that his experience in the war has alienated him from his past. Paul remains unable to resume his previous relationship with his family because the war has damaged his innocence and given him a new mindset that his family cannot possibly understand. In these scenes, Remarque essentially retreads the thematic material that he covers during Paul's visit home earlier in the novel. But he also demonstrates that the trauma Paul has suffered during the war has made it impossible for him to confront his feelings of loss, fear, and grief about his mother's illness; his worry for his mother is counterbalanced by the necessity of keeping his feelings at bay. At the same time, Remarque continues to emphasize Paul's essential goodness, showing his feelings of compassion in his decision to give the potato cakes to the prisoners and in his realization that the cakes should mean something to him since the effort that his ailing mother put into making them constituted a sacrifice.

Chapter Nine

Why do they never tell us that you are poor devils like us. . . .

(See QUOTATIONS, *p. 55)*

Summary

When Paul returns to the front, he finds Kat, Müller, Tjaden, and Kropp still alive and uninjured. He shares his potato cakes with them. There is excitement among the ranks: the kaiser, the emperor of Germany, is coming to see the army. In preparation for his visit, everything is cleaned thoroughly, and all the soldiers are given new clothes. But when the kaiser arrives, Paul and the others are disappointed to see that he is not a very remarkable man. After he leaves, the new clothes are taken away. Paul and his friends muse that if a certain thirty people in the world had said "no" to the war, it would not have happened. They conclude that wars are useful only for leaders who want to be in history books.

Paul volunteers to crawl into No Man's Land to gather information about the enemy's strength. On his way back, he becomes lost. A bombardment begins, and he knows that an attack is coming. He realizes that he must lie still and pretend to be dead, so he crawls into a shell hole to wait until the attack is over. An enemy soldier jumps into the shell hole with him, and Paul quickly stabs him. It is too light outside for Paul to make his way back, so he is forced to wait in the shell hole with the body. As he waits, he notices that the French soldier is not dead. Paul bandages the soldier's wounds and gives him water. The man takes several hours to die. It is the first time that Paul has killed someone in hand-to-hand combat, and the experience is pure agony.

Paul talks to the dead soldier, explaining that he did not want to kill him. Paul finds a picture of a woman and a little girl in the man's pocketbook. He reads what he can of the letters tucked inside. Every word plunges Paul deeper into guilt and pain. The dead man's name is Gérard Duval, and he was a printer by trade. Paul copies his address and resolves to send money to his family anonymously. As dark falls again, Paul's survival instinct reawakens. He knows that he will not fulfill his promise to the French soldier. He crawls back to his trench. Hours later, he confesses the experience of killing the printer to his comrades. Kat and Kropp draw his attention to their snipers enjoying the job of picking off enemy soldiers. They point out that he took no pleasure from his killing and, unlike the snipers, he had no choice; it was kill or be killed.

Analysis

In the previous chapter, Paul's experience with the Russian prisoners indicts the ethics of nationalism, and his discussion with his comrades early in this chapter continues in the same vein. They realize that the crushing irony of the war is that soldiers on both sides have been sent to fight based on exactly the same ideals. After this crucial realization, they find it impossible to determine who is right and who is wrong. In the end, nationalistic ideals are simply tools used by power- and status-hungry leaders to seduce citizens into supporting a war that does nothing but harm them. The war is useful only to very few men who never actually see combat. The worst senselessness of the matter, as Paul and his friends realize, is that millions of lives have been sacrificed by a decision made by fewer than thirty men.

Paul's entrance into No Man's Land as a spy finds him performing one of the most dangerous jobs in trench warfare. In No Man's Land, he is subject to fire from both sides. In a way, this symbolizes his rejection of nationalism—Paul has left the German ditch and entered the space controlled by no nation. This mission also provides the conditions for the most traumatic experience that Paul suffers in the novel. War is, of course, about killing, but, from a historical point of view, the killing in World War I was largely anonymous and conducted from far away, which is one of the reasons that the war, as the novel demonstrates, has such a dehumanizing effect. Now, for the first time, Paul kills a man in hand-to-hand combat. He sees the enemy face to face and is forced to understand the true cost of taking another human being's life. Gérard Duval is not a vague figure killed from a distance but an actual man, an individual just as the Russian soldiers were individuals. Shocked to see the terror in Duval's eyes, Paul is forced to realize that he is the source of the man's fear. He hesitates to read Gérard's name in his paybook because doing so will give his victim an even more concrete identity. He sees the life that he has destroyed and realizes that Gérard's wife and child are victims of his actions as well.

By the time Paul returns to the trenches, however, his instinct to separate himself from his emotions has kicked in, and he ceases to refer to Gérard as an individual. He calls him "the dead printer." Like Paul's detachment from his family and from his own condition, this emotional distancing is necessary. He cannot function as a soldier if he remains in the grip of grief and remorse that he experiences in the hours after killing Duval.

Chapter Ten

Summary

Paul, Tjaden, Müller, Kropp, Detering, and Kat have to guard a supply dump in an abandoned village. They use a concrete shelter for a dugout and take advantage of the opportunity to eat and sleep as much as they can. They take a large mahogany bed, mattresses, and blankets into their dugout because they rarely have access to such luxuries. They collect eggs and butter, and they have the luck to find two suckling pigs. They collect fresh vegetables and cook a grand dinner in a well-outfitted kitchen near the dugout. Paul makes pancakes while the others roast the pigs.

Unfortunately, the enemy sees the smoke rising from the chimney and bombs the house. As the attack begins, the men gather the food and make a dash for the dugout. Paul finishes cooking the pancakes while the bombs fall around him. Once he finishes, he grabs the plate of pancakes and manages to get to the dugout without losing a single one. The meal lasts four hours. Afterward, the men smoke cigars and cigarettes from the supply dump. They drink coffee and begin eating again before they end the night with cognac. They even feed a stray cat. The richness of the meal after such long deprivation causes them to suffer bouts of diarrhea all night.

For three weeks, the men live a "charmed life" before they are moved again. They take the bed, two armchairs, and the cat with them. While they are evacuating another village, Kropp and Paul are wounded by a falling shell. They find an ambulance wagon after struggling out of the zone of the shelling. Kropp has been wounded very close to his knee. He resolves to commit suicide if they amputate his leg. Paul's leg is broken and his arm is wounded. He and Kropp travel to the hospital in the same train car after bribing a sergeant-major with cigars.

Kropp develops a fever and must stop at the Catholic hospital nearby. Paul fakes an illness to go with him. Kropp's fever does not improve, so his leg has to be amputated from the thigh. Men die daily at the hospital. The amazing array of maiming wounds shows Paul that a hospital is the best place to learn what war is about. He wonders what will happen to his generation after the war.

Lewandowski, a forty-year-old soldier, is recuperating from a bad abdominal injury. He is excited that his wife is coming to visit him with the child she bore after he left to fight two years before. He wants to take his wife somewhere private, because he has not slept with her for two years. But before she arrives, he develops a fever, so he is confined to bed. When she arrives, she is nervous. Lewandowski explains what he wants, and she blushes furiously. The other patients tell her that social niceties can be dispensed with during wartime. Two men guard the door in case a doctor or one of the nuns arrives to check on a patient. Kropp holds the child and the other patients play cards and chat loudly with their backs to the couple while the couple makes love in Lewandowski's bed. The plan is carried off without a problem. Lewandowski's wife shares the food that she brought for her husband with the other patients.

Paul heals well. The hospital begins using paper bandages because the cloth ones have become scarce. Kropp's leg heals, but he is more solemn and less talkative than he used to be. Paul thinks that Kropp would have killed himself if he were not in a room with other patients. Paul receives leave to go home and finish healing. When his time at home is done, parting from his mother is even harder than the last time. She is weaker than before.

ANALYSIS

Compared to the grim tone of the preceding chapters, the scenes in the evacuated village are full of a certain bitter comedy. Paul and his friends make use of the opportunity to celebrate and live a charmed life because the chances to relax and become human are so few and far between. While Paul's decision to stay and finish his pancakes while bombs are falling around the kitchen seems insane, there is an appropriately demented logic to it: pancakes are his favorite dish, and he might well die the next day and thus never have them again.

There is, of course, a dark side to this scene. Paul and his friends are so used to being bombed and shot at that they can actually maintain the nerve to protect their meal during the bombardment. Moreover, they are so starved and hungry for real food that they are actually willing to risk their lives for it. At the same time, their antics while guarding the supply dump provide some hope. Remarque seems to imply that despite the ravages of war, small elements of humanity and human folly can survive the trenches.

The ride in the train with Kropp is also full of grim humor. Despite the dirtiness and coarseness of life in the trenches, Paul still suffers from a boyish modesty in his reluctance to tell one of the nurses that he needs to go to the bathroom. He doesn't want to lie in the bunks because the sheets are so clean and he is so dirty. In this way, Remarque demonstrates that though the war has in many ways destroyed Paul's innocence, Paul still retains a vestige of modesty in unfamiliar settings. The hospital scene also contains moments when Paul's boyish innocence shows signs of surviving. He throws a bottle at the door in order to force the nuns to shut it when they pray, but another man takes the blame because he has a medical condition that induces irrational, impetuous outbursts. Paul and the other patients react with glee when they discover this condition, because they know that they can commit all sorts of mischief.

The rest of the chapter continues to explore the extent to which humanity can survive the horrors of war. Lewandowski's feverish anticipation of his wife's visit demonstrates that human concerns can indeed weather the trenches. Moreover, the help that he gets in carrying out his plan shows the extraordinary level of familiarity and intimacy that soldiers share with one another, revealing the intense comradeship and understanding among the soldiers.

Another sign in this chapter of the brutality of war is the fact that the hospital is filled with men suffering from permanently disfiguring injuries. There are wards for soldiers suffering from poison gas injuries, amputations, blindness, and various other wounds. The hospital is a museum of the vast array of maiming and lethal injuries to which the human body is subject in modern warfare. The most succinct and shocking evidence of the human costs of war can be seen there. Remarque has Paul think that anyone who wants to learn about the war should visit a hospital. Paul is confident that such an experience would be a far better way to understand the actual meaning of war than to listen to idealistic rhetoric about patriotism and honor.

Chapter Eleven

Summary

The German army continues to weaken, but the war rages on. Paul and his comrades cease to count the weeks they have spent fighting. Paul compares war to a deadly disease like the flu, tuberculosis, or cancer. The men's thoughts are molded by "the changes of the days": when they are fighting, their thoughts go dead; when they are resting, their thoughts are good. Their prewar lives are "no longer valid" since the years before they joined the army have ceased to mean anything. Before, they were "coins of different provinces"; now, they are "melted down," and they all "bear the same stamp." They identify themselves as soldiers first, only second as individual men. They share an intimate, close bond with one another, like that of convicts sentenced to death. Survival requires their complete, unquestioning loyalty to one another.

Paul reflects that, for the soldiers, life is no more than the constant avoidance of death. They have to reduce themselves to the level of unthinking animals because instinct is their best weapon against unrelenting mortal danger. It helps them survive the horrendous conditions of trench warfare without losing their minds.

However, the war wears them down despite themselves. Eventually, they begin to crack. Detering sees a cherry tree blossoming one day. He takes a branch from the tree with him, reminding himself of his orchard at home, which is full of cherry trees. He deserts the army a few days later. Foolishly, he tries to go back home instead of fleeing to Holland, and he is captured and tried as a deserter. The Second Company never hears from him again. An enemy shoots Müller point-blank in the abdomen. His agonizingly painful death lasts half an hour. Paul receives Müller's boots, which once belonged to Kemmerich.

The war continues to go badly for the Germans. The quality of the soldiers' food worsens, and there is considerably less food. Dysentery strikes them with a vengeance. The Germans' weapons are worn and useless against the newer, more powerful artillery of their enemies. The new recruits are younger than ever before and have no training. Wounded men are sent back to fight before they are healed; even crippling physical defects do not save them from combat duty. Leer bleeds to death from a thigh wound. The summer of 1918 is horrific. Though they are obviously losing, the Germans keep fighting. Rumors of a possible end to the war make the soldiers more reluctant to return to the front lines.

Kat is wounded while returning with food that he has scavenged. Paul cannot leave him to find a stretcher because Kat is bleeding too much. Paul painstakingly carries him to the dressing station while shells crash around him. Kat is the only friend Paul has left in the army. When he reaches the station, still carrying Kat, he discovers that Kat has been hit in the head by a fragment from an exploding shell. Paul's dearest friend is dead.

Analysis

The final chapters of *All Quiet on the Western Front* are full of bitter irony. Even the battle-hardened soldiers are reaching the point of collapse. Their prewar lives have ceased to mean anything since they can no longer imagine a peacetime existence. Paul's comparison of the war to disease reflects an attack on the romantic ideals of warfare. Until now, he and his friends have avoided allowing the disease of war to infect them. At this point, however, the sickness is creeping into their minds and souls because it is becoming their only existence. They have ceased to think of themselves as anything other than soldiers fighting a hopeless conflict. They share an intense bond with one another, but it has now taken on the character of a bond between fellow convicts sentenced to death. The war has become a mental prison, as their country refuses to end the hostilities in the face of obvious evidence that it is losing the war badly.

Paul's analogy between minting coins and the effect of the war on veteran soldiers is also significant. It is true that he and his friends establish close bonds that far surpass any civilian or peacetime friendship. However, those bonds have been established through trial by fire. They have had to enter a crucible of unbelievable violence in order to form and solidify these friendships. In passing through this metaphorical fire, Paul and his company have been melded together, not so much against the enemy as against the harsh reality of war. The comparison of their relationships to those of convicts sentenced to death adds a sobering qualifier to the romanticized ideal of comradeship.

This analogy also reflects a grim self-understanding among Paul and his friends. Their individual identities no longer have any real meaning for them; rather, they see themselves as coins—de-individualized tokens used by the German army. All semblance of individuality has been "stamp[ed]" out, and the only identity that matters is that of German soldier. Paul and his company also resemble coins in that they are valuable only as means to an end—they are exchanged unsentimentally by those in charge of the war for the deaths of enemy soldiers or for a few yards of ground. Should they perish, they are easily replaced by another group of de-individualized tokens.

Paul and his friends know that Germany is losing the war. Rumors of peace are an endless torture to endure because they see the end in sight, yet they know that they might be killed when they return to the trenches, before the peace can be put into effect. Detering cracks under a particularly bad episode of shell shock, and he deserts. In the German army during World War I, the penalty of death was often applied to deserters. After several years of faithful service in the worst possible war in history, Detering meets his end as a traitor to his country. The irony is that he gives into homesickness for the very homeland that he is supposed to defend.

Chapter Twelve

Summary

In the autumn of 1918, after the bloodiest summer in Paul's wartime experience, Paul is the only living member of his original group of classmates. The war continues to rage, but now that the United States has joined the Allies, Germany's defeat is inevitable, only a matter of time. In light of the extreme privations suffered by both the German soldiers and the German people, it seems likely that if the war does not end soon, the German people will revolt against their leaders.

After inhaling poison gas, Paul is given fourteen days of leave to recuperate. A wave of intense desire to return home seizes him, but he is frightened because he has no goals; were he to return home, he wouldn't know what to do with himself. He fears that his generation will yield no survivors—that they will return home as living corpses, shells of human beings. He cannot bear the thought. Something that is essentially human in them must survive the years of bombardment, but he feels that his own life has been irrevocably destroyed.

After years of fighting, Paul is finally killed in October of 1918, on an extraordinarily quiet, peaceful day. The army report that day contains only one phrase: "All quiet on the Western Front." As Paul dies, his face is calm, "as though almost glad the end had come."

Analysis

Throughout *All Quiet on the Western Front,* Remarque portrays the soldiers as men constantly in flight from death. He often portrays this flight as a losing race against annihilation. The short, epilogue-like final chapter of the novel hammers this point home with savage irony. Paul and his friends survive nearly three years of trench warfare, only to die within months of the peace agreement. Paul dies in October 1918; the armistice that ended World War I was signed in November. Paul is also the last of the boys in his class. His death marks the end of a generation of young men from his town, who represent the lost generation as a whole. Some soldiers may have survived the war, but, in this chapter, Remarque portrays the conflict as having symbolically eradicated an entire generation.

To this point, Paul has narrated the events of *All Quiet on the Western Front.* The last two paragraphs of the novel, however, which detail Paul's death, are put forth by an unnamed, unspecified

SUMMARY & ANALYSIS

narrator on a separate page of the book. This passage marks the only time that the narration shifts out of the first person; additionally, the tense changes from present to past—the only time it does so beyond Paul's flashbacks. Remarque gives us no insight as to who this impromptu narrator is or at what point in time this reflection upon the story occurs, which helps to render the story timeless. The unemotional and impersonal nature of this concluding narration echoes the impersonality of the army report issued on the day of Paul's death. It is also consistent with the extraordinary omission of details about Paul's death—the narrator tells us simply that Paul "fell."

Paul's death is made even more senseless by the extraordinary peace and calm of the day on which he dies. The final indignity of the novel is perpetrated by the German army after Paul's death, as the army report that day reads: "All quiet on the Western Front"—the source of the novel's ironic and sardonic title. The carnage is so widespread in the war that the death of an individual soldier means nothing; a man can be shot down and the day still can be considered "[a]ll quiet." The war has systematically wiped out the humanity of the soldiers who fight in it; with Paul's death, the placid military report succeeds in eradicating his entire existence, as well as his mortal sacrifice for the empty ideals of nationalism and patriotism that forced him into the war.

Important Quotations Explained

1. This book is to be neither an accusation nor a confession, and least of all an adventure, for death is not an adventure to those who stand face to face with it. It will try simply to tell of a generation of men who, even though they may have escaped shells, were destroyed by the war.

This passage is the epigraph to the novel, telling the reader what the book is intended to be and mapping out some of its basic stylistic and thematic ground. The statement that the book is not "an adventure" separates it from most war novels in that it will dispense with elements of romance and excitement in favor of a stark, unsentimental presentation. The clarification that "death is not an adventure to those who stand face to face with it" suggests that books that tell stories of war as though they were exciting adventures do not do justice to the actual experience of soldiers. Death may be an adventure to the reader, sitting comfortably at home, but it is anything but that to the soldier who is actually confronted with the possibility of being blown to pieces at any moment. The epigraph also declares that the book will be the story of an entire generation, one "destroyed by the war" even if not actually killed off by it. The epigraph thus opens the novel's exploration of the effect of the war on those who fought it; war is a transforming force that not only injures and traumatizes but also annihilates selfhood.

There is friction, however, between the claim that the book will attempt "simply" to depict this annihilation and the claim that the book is not an accusation. *All Quiet on the Western Front* certainly takes a strong critical position against the war and against nationalist and ignorant figures like Kantorek and Himmelstoss. Perhaps the meaning of the epigraph is that the book will let events speak for themselves since they have not been embellished for the sake of some political goal. Still, it is hard to see the one-dimensional Kantorek as anything other than the object of accusation. The friction between realism and antiwar fervor found in the epigraph parallels an aesthetic tension in the novel, as Remarque tries to reconcile his hatred of the war with a need to create realistic characters who are more than mere punching bags.

2. For us lads of eighteen they ought to have been mediators and guides to the world of maturity . . . to the future . . . in our hearts we trusted them. The idea of authority, which they represented, was associated in our minds with a greater insight and a more humane wisdom. But the first death we saw shattered this belief. We had to recognize that our generation was more to be trusted than theirs. . . . The first bombardment showed us our mistake, and under it the world as they had taught it to us broke in pieces.

This quotation from Chapter One constitutes Paul's first and most direct exploration of how the older generation betrays the younger generation by convincing them to sacrifice their lives for the empty ideals of patriotism and honor. Paul says that authority figures from the older generation—parents, leaders, teachers such as Kantorek—should have been wise guides to the future and that, as boys, the young soldiers all assumed that they would be. But after the war began, the soldiers realized that the older generation had failed them, and Paul reacts to this failure with anger and disdain. He emphasizes that the older generation, which is constantly ready to criticize and ostracize young men for signs of cowardice or unpatriotic behavior but has not itself experienced the war, has no understanding of what the fighting is actually like. The younger generation must look to themselves to determine what is true and right because the older generation has proved itself incapable of teaching them.

3. At the sound of the first droning of the shells we rush back, in one part of our being, a thousand years. By the animal instinct that is awakened in us we are led and protected. It is not conscious; it is far quicker, much more sure, less fallible, than consciousness. . . . It is this other, this second sight in us, that has thrown us to the ground and saved us, without our knowing how. . . . We march up, moody or good-tempered soldiers—we reach the zone where the front begins and become on the instant human animals.

With these words, Paul describes, in Chapter Four, the psychological transformation that soldiers undergo when heading into battle. Paul observes this phenomenon as he and his comrades near the front on their mission to lay barbed wire. They cease to become men ("moody or good-tempered soldiers") and instead become beasts ("human animals"). To survive, it is necessary for the soldiers to sacrifice the thoughtful and analytical parts of their minds and rely instead wholly on animal instinct. Paul describes men who have been walking thoughtlessly along and suddenly thrown themselves to the ground just in time to avoid a shell, without having been consciously aware that a shell was approaching and without having intended to leap to avoid it. Paul calls this instinct a "second sight" and says that it is the only thing that enables soldiers to survive a battle. In this way, Paul implies that battles are animalistic and even subhuman, a large aspect of the devastation that the war wreaks on a soldier's humanity.

4. Just as we turn into animals when we go up to the line . . . so we turn into wags and loafers when we are resting. . . . We want to live at any price; so we cannot burden ourselves with feelings which, though they may be ornamental enough in peacetime, would be out of place here. Kemmerich is dead, Haie Westhus is dying . . . Martens has no legs anymore, Meyer is dead, Max is dead, Beyer is dead, Hammerling is dead . . . it is a damnable business, but what has it to do with us now—we live.

In this grim passage from Chapter Seven, Paul discusses the psychological process of how a soldier disconnects himself from his feelings in order to survive the terror of the war. After the bloody fighting, Paul and his friends are lying about enjoying a moment of relaxation and leisure, and have pushed their recent horrific experiences out of their minds. Paul says that terror can be survived only if one avoids thinking about it; otherwise, feelings of grief, fear, and despair would drive a man mad. Paul even looks upon those feelings with contempt, calling them "ornamental enough during peacetime" and implying that they are superfluous luxuries rather than essential components of the human experience. To help the reader understand the pressure that is always upon the soldier, Paul presents his appalling list of recent casualties, friends, and comrades who were either killed or badly injured in recent fighting. There is even a grotesque poetry to the list with the alliteration and rhyme of the names Martens, Meyer, Max, and Beyer, demonstrating the stoic attitude that Paul claims is necessary for survival.

5. Comrade, I did not want to kill you. . . . But you were only an idea to me before, an abstraction that lived in my mind and called forth its appropriate response. . . . I thought of your hand-grenades, of your bayonet, of your rifle; now I see your wife and your face and our fellowship. Forgive me, comrade. We always see it too late. Why do they never tell us that you are poor devils like us, that your mothers are just as anxious as ours, and that we have the same fear of death, and the same dying and the same agony—Forgive me, comrade; how could you be my enemy?

Paul utters these words in Chapter Nine to the corpse of Gérard Duval, the French soldier whom he has just killed. Paul realizes for the first time that, despite the dictates of nationalism, Duval is fundamentally no different from him. As Duval becomes a fully realized person in Paul's mind, as he thinks beyond the man's weapons to "your wife and your face and our fellowship," Paul observes, as he does in Chapter Eight among the Russian prisoners, that the war has forced men who are not enemies to fight each other. The propaganda campaigns waged by the opposing governments have convinced many men that their opponents are evil; as such, Paul initially conceives of the French soldier as "an abstraction"—the enemy. Once he understands Duval as a human being, the artificial divisions between the two men become irrelevant. Paul's sympathy for Duval's suffering is evident in his address of him as "comrade" and his reference to himself and Duval as "we" and "us," in opposition to the "they"—those in power, who attempt to deny the essential sameness of men such as Paul and Duval.

Key Facts

FULL TITLE

All Quiet on the Western Front (German: *Im Westen Nichts Neues*)

AUTHOR

Erich Maria Remarque

TYPE OF WORK

Novel

GENRES

War novel, historical fiction, novel of social protest

LANGUAGE

German

TIME AND PLACE WRITTEN

Late 1920s, Berlin

DATE OF FIRST PUBLICATION

1928

PUBLISHER

A. G. Ullstein in Germany; Little, Brown in the United States

NARRATOR

Paul Bäumer

POINT OF VIEW

Paul, the narrator, speaks primarily in the first person, often in the plural as he describes the collective experience of the soldiers immediately around him. He switches to the first person singular as he ruminates on his own thoughts and feelings about the war. The novel switches to the third person and an unnamed narrator for the two paragraphs following Paul's death.

TONE

Paul is Remarque's mouthpiece in the novel, and Paul's views can be considered those of Remarque.

TENSE

Present; occasionally past during flashbacks. The unnamed narrator at the end of the novel uses the past tense.

SETTINGS (TIME)

Late in World War I: 1917–1918

SETTINGS (PLACE)

The German/French front

PROTAGONIST

Paul

MAJOR CONFLICT

Paul and his friends have unwittingly entered a hellish war in which hope for survival is sullied by the knowledge that they have already been mentally scarred beyond recovery.

RISING ACTION

The wiring fatigue and the subsequent shelling in Chapter Four bring the men and the reader to the front for the first time in the story.

CLIMAX

Paul's killing of Gérard Duval in Chapter Nine is his first encounter with hand-to-hand combat and, in a sense, with the reality of war.

FALLING ACTION

Paul's remorse at killing Duval solidifies the novel's total rejection of the war and nationalist politics.

THEMES

The horror of war; the effect of war on the soldier; nationalism and political power

MOTIFS

The pressure of patriotic idealism; carnage and gore; animal instinct

SYMBOLS

Kemmerich's boots, which symbolize the cheapness of human life in the war

FORESHADOWING

There is little foreshadowing in the novel; the relentless carnage of the first ten chapters may foreshadow the death of Paul's group in Chapters 11 and 12.

Study Questions

1. *What are the main themes of* All Quiet on the Western Front?

Remarque's novel is a profound statement against war, focusing especially on the ravaging effects of war on the humanity of soldiers. Throughout Paul's narrative there are attacks on the romantic ideals of warfare. The novel dramatizes the disjunction between high-minded rhetoric about patriotism and honor and the actual horror of trench warfare. Remarque continually stresses that the soldiers are not fighting with the abstract ideals of patriotic spirit in mind; they are fighting for their survival. The matters of acquiring food, shelter, and clothing, in addition to avoiding gunfire and bombs, constitute their foremost concerns. Nothing in this novel makes the actual experience of war look attractive. Even the intense friendships between Paul and his fellow soldiers are tempered with the sobering reality that their bonds come at the high price of relentless suffering and terror.

Remarque also explores the gulfs in age and power that are widened by war; he portrays the war as the older generation's profound betrayal of the younger. Men of Paul's age entered the war under the heavy pressure of people they regarded as trusted authority figures. The very people who are supposed to guide them to their adulthood instead send them to their deaths with empty slogans of patriotic duty.

2. *How does Remarque portray the technological and military innovations of the war? How do those innovations affect the lives of the soldiers?*

Technological and military innovations such as poison gas, the machine gun, and trench warfare revolutionized combat during World War I, and Remarque effectively dramatizes how these innovations made the war bloodier, longer, and more costly. In almost every case, military innovations make the soldiers' lives more dangerous, while medical innovations lag increasingly far behind. Kemmerich, for instance, dies from complications from a relatively light wound. Glory and patriotism cease to be rational ideals in the conflict because advanced technology limits the effect that an individual soldier can have on the conflict and alienates him from the consequences of his actions. Life and death thus become meaningless. Whether or not a soldier dies in a bombardment is determined by chance or animal instinct and has nothing to do with the soldier's attitude toward the conflict.

3. *Think about the concept of enemies in war. Whom do Paul and his friends regard as their enemies?*

When Paul and his friends talk about enemies, they do not speak of the soldiers on the other side. Instead, they concentrate their hostility on Kantorek and Himmelstoss, their superiors and fellow countrymen. Paul and his classmates view Kantorek and other formerly trusted authority figures like him as the origin of their pointless suffering. These authority figures have sent them to war with the tragically false illusion that they were embarking on an exciting journey to fight for honor and glory. They view all common soldiers who are forced to fight in the trenches, regardless of their national origin, as victims. When Paul meets the Russian prisoners, he can hardly believe that they are his enemies—it is only the word of their respective leaders that has made them enemies. Because of the conflicts between more powerful men, Paul and the Russians are forced to kill and maim one another, even though they have more in common with one another than they do with their respective leaders.

4. *Why do Paul and men of his age group fear the end of the war as much as they fear the war itself?*

When Müller persistently questions his friends about their postwar plans, the younger men can give only vague answers. Older men mention their jobs and their families; they had concrete identities and social functions before the war. Younger men like Paul and his classmates had no such concrete identities. They entered the war when they were on the threshold of their adult lives and thus gained their identities as soldiers. Paul cannot even imagine any definite postwar goals. Many young men like him cannot view the war as a temporary interruption in their lives. Their experiences of the war are so shattering that they regard the prospect of functioning in a peacetime environment with a vague anxiety. For them, peace represents the unknown; the war, on the other hand, as terrible as it is, offers them some minimal comfort by virtue of their intimate familiarity with it. Whereas they know how to function as soldiers, Paul and the other young comrades cannot imagine functioning in civilian jobs. They have no experiences as adults that do not involve a day-to-day fight for survival and sanity.

How to Write Literary Analysis

The Literary Essay: A Step-by-Step Guide

When you read for pleasure, your only goal is enjoyment. You might find yourself reading to get caught up in an exciting story, to learn about an interesting time or place, or just to pass time. Maybe you're looking for inspiration, guidance, or a reflection of your own life. There are as many different, valid ways of reading a book as there are books in the world.

When you read a work of literature in an English class, however, you're being asked to read in a special way: you're being asked to perform *literary analysis*. To analyze something means to break it down into smaller parts and then examine how those parts work, both individually and together. Literary analysis involves examining all the parts of a novel, play, short story, or poem—elements such as character, setting, tone, and imagery—and thinking about how the author uses those elements to create certain effects.

A literary essay isn't a book review: you're not being asked whether or not you liked a book or whether you'd recommend it to another reader. A literary essay also isn't like the kind of book report you wrote when you were younger, where your teacher wanted you to summarize the book's action. A high school- or college-level literary essay asks, "How does this piece of literature actually work?" "How does it do what it does?" and, "Why might the author have made the choices he or she did?"

The Seven Steps

No one is born knowing how to analyze literature; it's a skill you learn and a process you can master. As you gain more practice with this kind of thinking and writing, you'll be able to craft a method that works best for you. But until then, here are seven basic steps to writing a well-constructed literary essay:

1. *Ask questions*
2. *Collect evidence*
3. *Construct a thesis*

4. *Develop and organize arguments*
5. *Write the introduction*
6. *Write the body paragraphs*
7. *Write the conclusion*

---

1. Ask Questions

When you're assigned a literary essay in class, your teacher will often provide you with a list of writing prompts. Lucky you! Now all you have to do is choose one. Do yourself a favor and pick a topic that interests you. You'll have a much better (not to mention easier) time if you start off with something you enjoy thinking about. If you are asked to come up with a topic by yourself, though, you might start to feel a little panicked. Maybe you have too many ideas—or none at all. Don't worry. Take a deep breath and start by asking yourself these questions:

- **What struck you?** Did a particular image, line, or scene linger in your mind for a long time? If it fascinated you, chances are you can draw on it to write a fascinating essay.
- **What confused you?** Maybe you were surprised to see a character act in a certain way, or maybe you didn't understand why the book ended the way it did. Confusing moments in a work of literature are like a loose thread in a sweater: if you pull on it, you can unravel the entire thing. Ask yourself why the author chose to write about that character or scene the way he or she did and you might tap into some important insights about the work as a whole.
- **Did you notice any patterns?** Is there a phrase that the main character uses constantly or an image that repeats throughout the book? If you can figure out how that pattern weaves through the work and what the significance of that pattern is, you've almost got your entire essay mapped out.
- **Did you notice any contradictions or ironies?** Great works of literature are complex; great literary essays recognize and explain those complexities. Maybe the title (*Happy Days*) totally disagrees with the book's subject matter (hungry orphans dying in the woods). Maybe the main character acts one way around his family and a completely different way around his friends and associates. If you can find a way to explain a work's contradictory elements, you've got the seeds of a great essay.

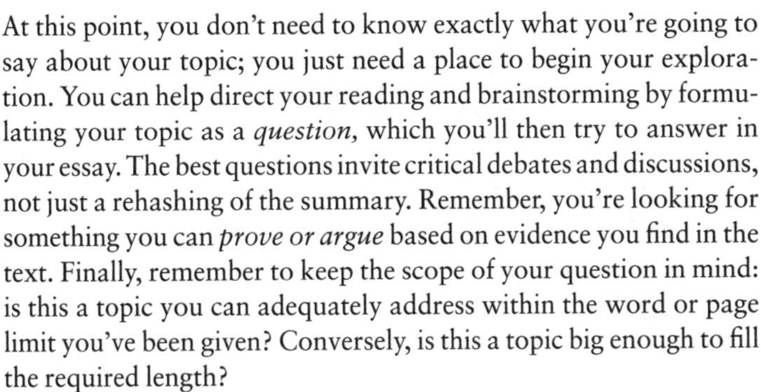

At this point, you don't need to know exactly what you're going to say about your topic; you just need a place to begin your exploration. You can help direct your reading and brainstorming by formulating your topic as a *question,* which you'll then try to answer in your essay. The best questions invite critical debates and discussions, not just a rehashing of the summary. Remember, you're looking for something you can *prove or argue* based on evidence you find in the text. Finally, remember to keep the scope of your question in mind: is this a topic you can adequately address within the word or page limit you've been given? Conversely, is this a topic big enough to fill the required length?

GOOD QUESTIONS

"Are Romeo and Juliet's parents responsible for the deaths of their children?"

"Why do pigs keep showing up in LORD OF THE FLIES*?"*

"Are Dr. Frankenstein and his monster alike? How?"

BAD QUESTIONS

"What happens to Scout in TO KILL A MOCKINGBIRD*?"*

"What do the other characters in JULIUS CAESAR *think about Caesar?"*

"How does Hester Prynne in THE SCARLET LETTER *remind me of my sister?"*

---

2. COLLECT EVIDENCE

Once you know what question you want to answer, it's time to scour the book for things that will help you answer the question. Don't worry if you don't know what you want to say yet—right now you're just collecting ideas and material and letting it all percolate. Keep track of passages, symbols, images, or scenes that deal with your topic. Eventually, you'll start making connections between these examples and your thesis will emerge.

Here's a brief summary of the various parts that compose each and every work of literature. These are the elements that you will analyze in your essay, and which you will offer as evidence to support your arguments. For more on the parts of literary works, see the Glossary of Literary Terms at the end of this section.

ELEMENTS OF STORY These are the *whats* of the work—what happens, where it happens, and to whom it happens.

- **Plot:** All of the events and actions of the work.
- **Character:** The people who act and are acted upon in a literary work. The main character of a work is known as the *protagonist.*
- **Conflict:** The central tension in the work. In most cases, the protagonist wants something, while opposing forces (antagonists) hinder the protagonist's progress.
- **Setting:** When and where the work takes place. Elements of setting include location, time period, time of day, weather, social atmosphere, and economic conditions.
- **Narrator:** The person telling the story. The narrator may straightforwardly report what happens, convey the subjective opinions and perceptions of one or more characters, or provide commentary and opinion in his or her own voice.
- **Themes:** The main idea or message of the work—usually an abstract idea about people, society, or life in general. A work may have many themes, which may be in tension with one another.

ELEMENTS OF STYLE These are the *hows*—how the characters speak, how the story is constructed, and how language is used throughout the work.

- **Structure and organization:** How the parts of the work are assembled. Some novels are narrated in a linear, chronological fashion, while others skip around in time. Some plays follow a traditional three- or five-act structure, while others are a series of loosely connected scenes. Some authors deliberately leave gaps in their works, leaving readers to puzzle out the missing information. A work's structure and organization can tell you a lot about the kind of message it wants to convey.
- **Point of view:** The perspective from which a story is told. In *first-person point of view,* the narrator involves him or herself in the story. ("I went to the store"; "We watched in horror as the bird slammed into the window.") A first-person narrator is usually the protagonist of the work, but not always. In *third-person point of view,* the narrator does not participate

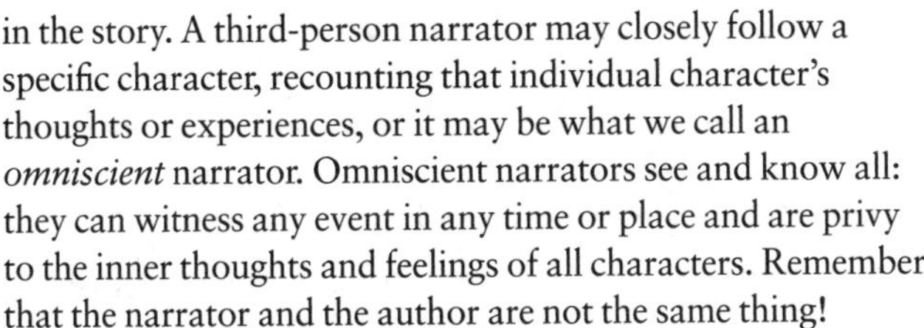

in the story. A third-person narrator may closely follow a specific character, recounting that individual character's thoughts or experiences, or it may be what we call an *omniscient* narrator. Omniscient narrators see and know all: they can witness any event in any time or place and are privy to the inner thoughts and feelings of all characters. Remember that the narrator and the author are not the same thing!

- **Diction:** Word choice. Whether a character uses dry, clinical language or flowery prose with lots of exclamation points can tell you a lot about his or her attitude and personality.
- **Syntax:** Word order and sentence construction. Syntax is a crucial part of establishing an author's narrative voice. Ernest Hemingway, for example, is known for writing in very short, straightforward sentences, while James Joyce characteristically wrote in long, incredibly complicated lines.
- **Tone:** The mood or feeling of the text. Diction and syntax often contribute to the tone of a work. A novel written in short, clipped sentences that use small, simple words might feel brusque, cold, or matter-of-fact.
- **Imagery:** Language that appeals to the senses, representing things that can be seen, smelled, heard, tasted, or touched.
- **Figurative language:** Language that is not meant to be interpreted literally. The most common types of figurative language are *metaphors* and *similes,* which compare two unlike things in order to suggest a similarity between them—for example, "All the world's a stage," or "The moon is like a ball of green cheese." (Metaphors say one thing *is* another thing; similes claim that one thing is *like* another thing.)

---

3. Construct a Thesis

When you've examined all the evidence you've collected and know how you want to answer the question, it's time to write your thesis statement. A *thesis* is a claim about a work of literature that needs to be supported by evidence and arguments. The thesis statement is the heart of the literary essay, and the bulk of your paper will be spent trying to prove this claim. A good thesis will be:

- **Arguable.** "*The Great Gatsby* describes New York society in the 1920s" isn't a thesis—it's a fact.

- **Provable through textual evidence.** "*Hamlet* is a confusing but ultimately very well-written play" is a weak thesis because it offers the writer's personal opinion about the book. Yes, it's arguable, but it's not a claim that can be proved or supported with examples taken from the play itself.
- **Surprising.** "Both George and Lenny change a great deal in *Of Mice and Men*" is a weak thesis because it's obvious. A really strong thesis will argue for a reading of the text that is not immediately apparent.
- **Specific.** "Dr. Frankenstein's monster tells us a lot about the human condition" is *almost* a really great thesis statement, but it's still too vague. What does the writer mean by "a lot"? *How* does the monster tell us so much about the human condition?

Good Thesis Statements

Question: In *Romeo and Juliet*, which is more powerful in shaping the lovers' story: fate or foolishness?

Thesis: "Though Shakespeare defines Romeo and Juliet as 'star-crossed lovers' and images of stars and planets appear throughout the play, a closer examination of that celestial imagery reveals that the stars are merely witnesses to the characters' foolish activities and not the causes themselves."

Question: How does the bell jar function as a symbol in Sylvia Plath's *The Bell Jar*?

Thesis: "A bell jar is a bell-shaped glass that has three basic uses: to hold a specimen for observation, to contain gases, and to maintain a vacuum. The bell jar appears in each of these capacities in *The Bell Jar*, Plath's semi-autobiographical novel, and each appearance marks a different stage in Esther's mental breakdown."

Question: Would Piggy in *The Lord of the Flies* make a good island leader if he were given the chance?

Thesis: "Though the intelligent, rational, and innovative Piggy has the mental characteristics of a good leader, he ultimately lacks the social skills necessary to be an effective one. Golding emphasizes this point by giving Piggy a foil in the charismatic Jack, whose magnetic personality allows him to capture and wield power effectively, if not always wisely."

4. Develop and Organize Arguments

The reasons and examples that support your thesis will form the middle paragraphs of your essay. Since you can't really write your thesis statement until you know how you'll structure your argument, you'll probably end up working on steps 3 and 4 at the same time.

There's no single method of argumentation that will work in every context. One essay prompt might ask you to compare and contrast two characters, while another asks you to trace an image through a given work of literature. These questions require different kinds of answers and therefore different kinds of arguments. Below, we'll discuss three common kinds of essay prompts and some strategies for constructing a solid, well-argued case.

Types of Literary Essays

- **Compare and contrast**

  Compare and contrast the characters of Huck and Jim in THE ADVENTURES OF HUCKLEBERRY FINN.

  Chances are you've written this kind of essay before. In an academic literary context, you'll organize your arguments the same way you would in any other class. You can either go *subject by subject* or *point by point*. In the former, you'll discuss one character first and then the second. In the latter, you'll choose several traits (attitude toward life, social status, images and metaphors associated with the character) and devote a paragraph to each. You may want to use a mix of these two approaches—for example, you may want to spend a paragraph a piece broadly sketching Huck's and Jim's personalities before transitioning into a paragraph or two that describes a few key points of comparison. This can be a highly effective strategy if you want to make a counterintuitive argument—that, despite seeming to be totally different, the two objects being compared are actually similar in a very important way (or vice versa). Remember that your essay should reveal something fresh or unexpected about the text, so think beyond the obvious parallels and differences.

- **Trace**

  Choose an image—for example, birds, knives, or eyes—and trace that image throughout MACBETH.

  Sounds pretty easy, right? All you need to do is read the play, underline every appearance of a knife in *Macbeth*, and then list them in your essay in the order they appear, right? Well, not exactly. Your teacher doesn't want a simple catalog of examples. He or she wants to see you make *connections* between those examples—that's the difference between summarizing and analyzing. In the *Macbeth* example above, think about the different contexts in which knives appear in the play and to what effect. In *Macbeth*, there are real knives and imagined knives; knives that kill and knives that simply threaten. Categorize and classify your examples to give them some order. Finally, always keep the overall effect in mind. After you choose and analyze your examples, you should come to some greater understanding about the work, as well as your chosen image, symbol, or phrase's role in developing the major themes and stylistic strategies of that work.

- **Debate**

  Is the society depicted in 1984 *good for its citizens?*

In this kind of essay, you're being asked to debate a moral, ethical, or aesthetic issue regarding the work. You might be asked to judge a character or group of characters (*Is Caesar responsible for his own demise?*) or the work itself (*Is* JANE EYRE *a feminist novel?*). For this kind of essay, there are two important points to keep in mind. First, don't simply base your arguments on your personal feelings and reactions. Every literary essay expects you to read and analyze the work, so search for evidence in the text. What do characters in *1984* have to say about the government of Oceania? What images does Orwell use that might give you a hint about his attitude toward the government? As in any debate, you also need to make sure that you define all the necessary terms before you begin to argue your case. What does it mean to be a "good" society? What makes a novel "feminist"? You should define your terms right up front, in the first paragraph after your introduction.

Second, remember that strong literary essays make contrary and surprising arguments. Try to think outside the box. In the *1984* example above, it seems like the obvious answer would be no, the totalitarian society depicted in Orwell's novel is *not* good for its citizens. But can you think of any arguments for the opposite side? Even if your final assertion is that the novel depicts a cruel, repressive, and therefore harmful society, acknowledging and responding to the counterargument will strengthen your overall case.

5. Write the Introduction

Your introduction sets up the entire essay. It's where you present your topic and articulate the particular issues and questions you'll be addressing. It's also where you, as the writer, introduce yourself to your readers. A persuasive literary essay immediately establishes its writer as a knowledgeable, authoritative figure.

An introduction can vary in length depending on the overall length of the essay, but in a traditional five-paragraph essay it should be no longer than one paragraph. However long it is, your introduction needs to:

- **Provide any necessary context.** Your introduction should situate the reader and let him or her know what to expect. What book are you discussing? Which characters? What topic will you be addressing?
- **Answer the "So what?" question.** Why is this topic important, and why is your particular position on the topic noteworthy? Ideally, your introduction should pique the reader's interest by suggesting how your argument is surprising or otherwise counterintuitive. Literary essays make unexpected connections and reveal less-than-obvious truths.
- **Present your thesis.** This usually happens at or very near the end of your introduction.
- **Indicate the shape of the essay to come.** Your reader should finish reading your introduction with a good sense of the scope of your essay as well as the path you'll take toward proving your thesis. You don't need to spell out every step, but you do need to suggest the organizational pattern you'll be using.

Your introduction should not:

- **Be vague.** Beware of the two killer words in literary analysis: *interesting* and *important*. Of course the work, question, or example is interesting and important—that's why you're writing about it!
- **Open with any grandiose assertions.** Many student readers think that beginning their essays with a flamboyant statement such as, "Since the dawn of time, writers have been fascinated with the topic of free will," makes them

sound important and commanding. You know what? It actually sounds pretty amateurish.

- **Wildly praise the work.** Another typical mistake student writers make is extolling the work or author. Your teacher doesn't need to be told that "Shakespeare is perhaps the greatest writer in the English language." You can mention a work's reputation in passing—by referring to *The Adventures of Huckleberry Finn* as "Mark Twain's enduring classic," for example—but don't make a point of bringing it up unless that reputation is key to your argument.
- **Go off-topic.** Keep your introduction streamlined and to the point. Don't feel the need to throw in all kinds of bells and whistles in order to impress your reader—just get to the point as quickly as you can, without skimping on any of the required steps.

---

6. Write the Body Paragraphs

Once you've written your introduction, you'll take the arguments you developed in step 4 and turn them into your body paragraphs. The organization of this middle section of your essay will largely be determined by the argumentative strategy you use, but no matter how you arrange your thoughts, your body paragraphs need to do the following:

- **Begin with a strong topic sentence.** Topic sentences are like signs on a highway: they tell the reader where they are and where they're going. A good topic sentence not only alerts readers to what issue will be discussed in the following paragraph but also gives them a sense of what argument will be made *about* that issue. "Rumor and gossip play an important role in *The Crucible*" isn't a strong topic sentence because it doesn't tell us very much. "The community's constant gossiping creates an environment that allows false accusations to flourish" is a much stronger topic sentence—it not only tells us *what* the paragraph will discuss (gossip) but *how* the paragraph will discuss the topic (by showing how gossip creates a set of conditions that leads to the play's climactic action).
- **Fully and completely develop a single thought.** Don't skip around in your paragraph or try to stuff in too much material. Body paragraphs are like bricks: each individual

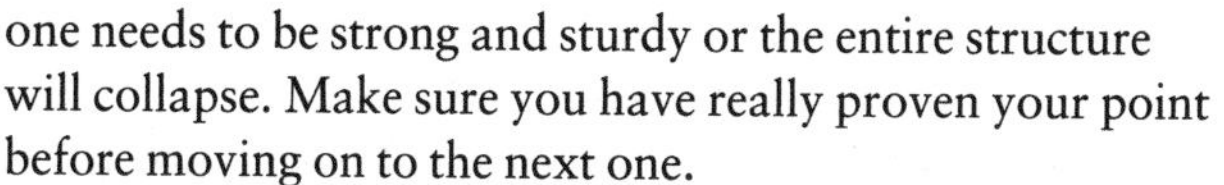

one needs to be strong and sturdy or the entire structure will collapse. Make sure you have really proven your point before moving on to the next one.

- **Use transitions effectively.** Good literary essay writers know that each paragraph must be clearly and strongly linked to the material around it. Think of each paragraph as a response to the one that precedes it. Use transition words and phrases such as *however, similarly, on the contrary, therefore,* and *furthermore* to indicate what kind of response you're making.

---

7. Write the Conclusion

Just as you used the introduction to ground your readers in the topic before providing your thesis, you'll use the conclusion to quickly summarize the specifics learned thus far and then hint at the broader implications of your topic. A good conclusion will:

- **Do more than simply restate the thesis.** If your thesis argued that *The Catcher in the Rye* can be read as a Christian allegory, don't simply end your essay by saying, "And that is why *The Catcher in the Rye* can be read as a Christian allegory." If you've constructed your arguments well, this kind of statement will just be redundant.
- **Synthesize the arguments, not summarize them.** Similarly, don't repeat the details of your body paragraphs in your conclusion. The reader has already read your essay, and chances are it's not so long that they've forgotten all your points by now.
- **Revisit the "So what?" question.** In your introduction, you made a case for why your topic and position are important. You should close your essay with the same sort of gesture. What do your readers know now that they didn't know before? How will that knowledge help them better appreciate or understand the work overall?
- **Move from the specific to the general.** Your essay has most likely treated a very specific element of the work—a single character, a small set of images, or a particular passage. In your conclusion, try to show how this narrow discussion has wider implications for the work overall. If your essay on *To Kill a Mockingbird* focused on the character of Boo Radley, for example, you might want to include a bit in your

conclusion about how he fits into the novel's larger message about childhood, innocence, or family life.

- **Stay relevant.** Your conclusion should suggest new directions of thought, but it shouldn't be treated as an opportunity to pad your essay with all the extra, interesting ideas you came up with during your brainstorming sessions but couldn't fit into the essay proper. Don't attempt to stuff in unrelated queries or too many abstract thoughts.
- **Avoid making overblown closing statements.** A conclusion should open up your highly specific, focused discussion, but it should do so without drawing a sweeping lesson about life or human nature. Making such observations may be part of the point of reading, but it's almost always a mistake in essays, where these observations tend to sound overly dramatic or simply silly.

A+ Essay Checklist

Congratulations! If you've followed all the steps we've outlined above, you should have a solid literary essay to show for all your efforts. What if you've got your sights set on an A+? To write the kind of superlative essay that will be rewarded with a perfect grade, keep the following rubric in mind. These are the qualities that teachers expect to see in a truly A+ essay. How does yours stack up?

- ✓ Demonstrates a thorough understanding of the book
- ✓ Presents an original, compelling argument
- ✓ Thoughtfully analyzes the text's formal elements
- ✓ Uses appropriate and insightful examples
- ✓ Structures ideas in a logical and progressive order
- ✓ Demonstrates a mastery of sentence construction, transitions, grammar, spelling, and word choice

Suggested Essay Topics

1. *According to the text, how does war empower petty, power-hungry men? Think especially about Himmelstoss. How do the other characters cope with their forced subordination?*

2. *In what ways does the novel critique the romantic rhetoric of war, honor, and patriotism? How might this critique extend to nineteenth-century ideas of nationalism? Think especially about the soldiers' reaction to Kantorek's letter.*

3. *What is Paul like as a character? Has the brutality of war completely stripped away his humanity, or does he retain vestiges of his old self?*

4. *Discuss how the goals of the novel, as stated by the epigraph or suggested by the text, affect the work's form and style. Does Remarque compromise his realistic style in order to deliver a message? Is Kantorek too one-dimensional a character?*

A+ Student Essay

How does *All Quiet on the Western Front* differ from a traditional coming-of-age novel, which charts the protagonist's growth as an individual?

Erich Remarque's *All Quiet on the Western Front* describes the young German soldier Paul Bäumer's experiences in World War I, from his training to his death in battle. However, rather than show us how Paul grows as an individual, developing his own ideas and value system, the novel instead shows how Paul—along with his fellow soldiers—survives the war by doing precisely the opposite. The horrors of battle force the soldiers to develop animalistic instincts and a pack-like bond. There is no place for individuals in war, and therefore no place for a traditional coming-of-age tale.

The opening pages of *All Quiet on the Western Front* emphasize how war dissolves individual men into a single, collective identity. Most fictional autobiographies are narrated in the first-person singular, as the protagonist recounts his or her development from a child into an adult subject. However, Paul begins his tale by speaking not about himself but about his unit, using the third-person plural pronoun "we." From the beginning, Paul is assimilated into the mass—a mass, moreover, that has been reduced to bodily functions and animal appetites. The third-person plural resonates throughout this first chapter as the soldiers operate as a single unit, motivated by the same communal desires: "we were growing impatient," "we got excited," "we were in just the right mood." The emotions that drive this group arise not from elevated sentiments but rather from the most fundamental animal needs. What unite the soldiers, the reader discovers, are not the head and the heart, but the stomach and the intestines—full bellies and general latrines.

In order to survive the horrors of war, Paul must perform a type of human sacrifice, eradicating his feelings and sensibilities so that all that remains is, as he puts it, a "human animal." In Chapter Seven, Paul describes how he must distance himself from his emotions and rely solely on automatic, animal instincts. In war, that which makes a person human can cost a soldier his sanity, if not his life. As Paul puts it, emotions—the qualities that make up individual human experience—are "ornamental enough during peacetime." A soldier must not only discard his immediate emotional reactions to survive, but he must also sever his ties to the past and plans for the future. The war becomes the focal point of his universe, and his identity before or after becomes an irrelevant distraction. The only things that matter on the battlefield are the immediate physical stimuli: blood, hunger, bullets, and pain.

The soldiers are not only animal-like in the way that they reject human emotions and live completely in the present: The violent ways they struggle for power through the exercise of brute force also make them beastly. In explaining how a seemingly subservient postman like Himmelstoss could turn into such a bully as a drill-sergeant, Paul's friend and fellow soldier, Kat, points out that the army's power structure brings out the animals hidden within human beings. Human civilization is just a veneer, Kat argues, and humans have more in common with the animal kingdom than they would like to admit. When he participates in viciously swarming the unsuspecting Himmelstoss, Paul himself illustrates Kat's point by engaging in behavior more appropriate to a savage herd animal than to a rational human individual.

If, as Kat argues, it is the structure of the army that is responsible for bringing out the soldiers' collective-minded, animal side, then perhaps armistice will enable these men to recapture their individual humanities. Yet for Paul, the prospect of armistice does not seem to promise a return to the human community. Paul imagines that any return to civilized society will be a profoundly alienating experience, one in which "men will not understand" him and in which veterans of his generation will become "superfluous." His war experience has excluded Paul from the general civilian community, and now the only form of community he can rely on is the animalism of his fellow soldiers. As Paul voices his fear that his generation will fail to "adapt" to the civilized world, his use of Darwinian language draws a final link between the human and animal kingdoms, suggesting that war not only turns the soldier from a human individual into an animal, but that by doing so it ineradicably alters the individual's ability to relate to other humans.

Glossary of Literary Terms

ANTAGONIST
: The entity that acts to frustrate the goals of the *protagonist*. The antagonist is usually another *character* but may also be a nonhuman force.

ANTIHERO / ANTIHEROINE
: A *protagonist* who is not admirable or who challenges notions of what should be considered admirable.

CHARACTER
: A person, animal, or any other thing with a personality that appears in a *narrative*.

CLIMAX
: The moment of greatest intensity in a text or the major turning point in the *plot*.

CONFLICT
: The central struggle that moves the *plot* forward. The conflict can be the *protagonist*'s struggle against fate, nature, society, or another person.

FIRST-PERSON POINT OF VIEW
: A literary style in which the *narrator* tells the story from his or her own *point of view* and refers to himself or herself as "I." The narrator may be an active participant in the story or just an observer.

HERO / HEROINE
: The principal *character* in a literary work or *narrative*.

IMAGERY
: Language that brings to mind sense-impressions, representing things that can be seen, smelled, heard, tasted, or touched.

MOTIF
: A recurring idea, structure, contrast, or device that develops or informs the major *themes* of a work of literature.

NARRATIVE
: A story.

NARRATOR
The person (sometimes a *character*) who tells a story; the *voice* assumed by the writer. The narrator and the author of the work of literature are not the same person.

PLOT
The arrangement of the events in a story, including the sequence in which they are told, the relative emphasis they are given, and the causal connections between events.

POINT OF VIEW
The *perspective* that a *narrative* takes toward the events it describes.

PROTAGONIST
The main *character* around whom the story revolves.

SETTING
The location of a *narrative* in time and space. Setting creates mood or atmosphere.

SUBPLOT
A secondary *plot* that is of less importance to the overall story but may serve as a point of contrast or comparison to the main plot.

SYMBOL
An object, *character,* figure, or color that is used to represent an abstract idea or concept. Unlike an *emblem,* a symbol may have different meanings in different contexts.

SYNTAX
The way the words in a piece of writing are put together to form lines, phrases, or clauses; the basic structure of a piece of writing.

THEME
A fundamental and universal idea explored in a literary work.

TONE
The author's attitude toward the subject or *characters* of a story or poem or toward the reader.

VOICE
An author's individual way of using language to reflect his or her own personality and attitudes. An author communicates voice through *tone, diction,* and *syntax*.

A Note on Plagiarism

Plagiarism—presenting someone else's work as your own—rears its ugly head in many forms. Many students know that copying text without citing it is unacceptable. But some don't realize that even if you're not quoting directly, but instead are paraphrasing or summarizing, *it is plagiarism* unless you cite the source.

Here are the most common forms of plagiarism:

- Using an author's phrases, sentences, or paragraphs without citing the source
- Paraphrasing an author's ideas without citing the source
- Passing off another student's work as your own

How do you steer clear of plagiarism? You should *always* acknowledge all words and ideas that aren't your own by using quotation marks around verbatim text or citations like footnotes and endnotes to note another writer's ideas. For more information on how to give credit when credit is due, ask your teacher for guidance or visit www.sparknotes.com.

Review & Resources

Quiz

1. Who is the first of Paul's classmates to die during the war?

   A. Joseph Behm
   B. Kropp
   C. Müller
   D. Kemmerich

2. Whose boots does Müller want?

   A. Kropp's
   B. Paul's
   C. Kemmerich's
   D. Tjaden's

3. Which character has a knack for finding food?

   A. Kropp
   B. Kat
   C. Paul
   D. Tjaden

4. For what medical condition that plagues Tjaden does Himmelstoss devise a humiliating cure?

   A. Bad breath
   B. Gas
   C. A hernia
   D. Bed-wetting

5. From what illness does Paul's mother suffer?

   A. Cancer
   B. Tuberculosis
   C. German measles
   D. Trench foot

6. What did Kantorek encourage his students to do about the war?

   A. Avoid it at all costs.
   B. Fight if conscripted; otherwise live at peace.
   C. Emigrate to America.
   D. Patriotically enlist at once.

7. With what friend is Paul hospitalized?

   A. Kemmerich
   B. Kropp
   C. Kat
   D. Tjaden

8. How long before the Armistice does Paul die?

   A. A year or more
   B. Six months
   C. Four months
   D. One month

9. Who dies as Paul carries him to safety?

   A. Kat
   B. Kropp
   C. Müller
   D. Haie Westhus

10. What prompts Detering to desert?

    A. A letter from his wife
    B. The loss of an arm
    C. The sight of cherry trees
    D. The scent of the ocean

11. What nationality are the prisoners whom Paul befriends?

    A. American
    B. Russian
    C. English
    D. French

12. What nationality is the soldier whom Paul stabs to death?

    A. American
    B. Russian
    C. English
    D. French

13. Where does Paul choose to spend his leave?

    A. At home with his family
    B. On the Italian coast
    C. In Berlin
    D. In Paris

14. According to Kat, what would happen if the enlisted men and the officers were all given the same pay?

    A. The army would be far more successful.
    B. The enlisted men would end up giving orders.
    C. The war would end immediately.
    D. The war would never end.

15. According to Kropp, how should disagreements between nations be resolved?

    A. By drawing lots
    B. The leaders should fight it out with clubs.
    C. The leaders should lock themselves in a room until they agree.
    D. By fighting wars

16. Who kills the goose?

    A. Paul
    B. Kropp
    C. Tjaden
    D. Kat

17. Which character most loathes Himmelstoss?

    A. Paul
    B. Tjaden
    C. Kat
    D. Müller

18. Which character is the last to die?

    A. Müller
    B. Kat
    C. Paul
    D. Kemmerich

19. What happens when half the company is killed at the beginning of the novel?

    A. The survivors receive double rations and enjoy a large meal.
    B. The survivors are emotionally devastated.
    C. The survivors are chastised by the general for letting their comrades die.
    D. The survivors steal the dead men's clothes.

20. What inventions made World War I so different from previous wars?

    A. The hot-air balloon and the cannon
    B. The airplane, the machine gun, and the hydrogen bomb
    C. The machine gun, the hydrogen bomb, and the grenade
    D. The airplane, the machine gun, the grenade, and poison gas

21. In what year was the novel first published in English?

    A. 1919
    B. 1923
    C. 1927
    D. 1929

22. What is the term for the long ditches from which the armies attack one another?

    A. Barricades
    B. Trenches
    C. Furrows
    D. Shell slides

23. What nationality is the girl with whom Paul sleeps?

A. American
B. Russian
C. French
D. German

24. What does the army report say on the day Paul is killed?

A. "All quiet on the Western Front"
B. "Brave soldier fallen"
C. "19,239 dead"
D. Nothing; the war officially ends just before Paul is killed.

25. What is Kropp's first name?

A. Paul
B. Rainer
C. Thorsten
D. Albert

ANSWER KEY

1: A; 2: C; 3: B; 4: D; 5: A; 6: D; 7: B; 8: D; 9: A; 10: C; 11: B; 12: D; 13: A; 14: C; 15: B; 16: D; 17: B; 18: C; 19: A; 20: D; 21: D; 22: B; 23: C; 24: A; 25: D

Suggestions for Further Reading

BARKER, CHRISTINE R. and R. W. LAST. *Erich Maria Remarque.* New York: Barnes & Noble, 1979.

BLOOM, HAROLD, ed. ALL QUIET ON THE WESTERN FRONT: *Modern Critical Interpretations.* New York: Chelsea House Publishers, 2000.

CHICKERING, ROGER. *Imperial Germany and the Great War, 1914–1918.* New York: Cambridge University Press, 2nd edition, 2004.

FIRDA, RICHARD ARTHUR. ALL QUIET ON THE WESTERN FRONT: *Literary Analysis and Cultural Context.* New York: Twayne, 1993.

GILBERT, JULIE GOLDSMITH. *Opposite Attraction: Erich Maria Remarque and Paulette Goddard.* New York: Pantheon Books, 1995.

MURDOCH, BRIAN. *The Novels of Erich Maria Remarque: Sparks of Life.* Elizabethtown, NY: Camden House, 2006.

REMARQUE, ERICH MARIA. *The Road Back.* Trans. A. W. Wheen. New York: Fawcett Books, 1998.

SCHWARZ, WILHELM J. *War and the Mind of Germany.* Frankfurt: Peter Lang, 1975.

TIMS, HILTON. *Erich Maria Remarque: The Last Romantic.* New York: Carroll & Graf Publishers, 2004.

SparkNotes Literature Guides

1984
The Adventures of Huckleberry Finn
The Adventures of Tom Sawyer
The Aeneid
All Quiet on the Western Front
And Then There Were None
Angela's Ashes
Animal Farm
Anna Karenina
Anne of Green Gables
Anthem
As I Lay Dying
The Awakening
The Bean Trees
Beloved
Beowulf
Billy Budd
Black Boy
Bless Me, Ultima
The Bluest Eye
Brave New World
The Brothers Karamazov
The Call of the Wild
Candide
The Canterbury Tales
Catch-22
The Catcher in the Rye
The Chocolate War
The Chosen
Cold Sassy Tree
The Color Purple
The Count of Monte Cristo
Crime and Punishment
The Crucible
Cry, the Beloved Country
Cyrano de Bergerac
David Copperfield
Death of a Salesman
Death of Socrates
Diary of a Young Girl
A Doll's House
Don Quixote
Dr. Faustus
Dr. Jekyll and Mr. Hyde
Dracula
Edith Hamilton's Mythology
Emma
Ethan Frome
Fahrenheit 451
A Farewell to Arms
The Fellowship of the Rings
Flowers for Algernon
For Whom the Bell Tolls
The Fountainhead
Frankenstein
The Giver
The Glass Menagerie
The Good Earth
The Grapes of Wrath
Great Expectations
The Great Gatsby
Grendel
Gulliver's Travels
Hamlet
The Handmaid's Tale
Hard Times
Heart of Darkness
Henry IV, Part I
Henry V
Hiroshima
The Hobbit
The House on Mango Street
I Know Why the Caged Bird Sings
The Iliad
The Importance of Being Earnest
Inferno
Invisible Man
Jane Eyre
Johnny Tremain
The Joy Luck Club
Julius Caesar
The Jungle
The Killer Angels
King Lear
The Last of the Mohicans
Les Misérables
A Lesson Before Dying
Little Women
Lord of the Flies
Macbeth
Madame Bovary
The Merchant of Venice
A Midsummer Night's Dream
Moby-Dick
Much Ado About Nothing
My Ántonia
Narrative of the Life of Frederick Douglass
Native Son
The New Testament
Night
The Odyssey
Oedipus Plays
Of Mice and Men
The Old Man and the Sea
The Old Testament
Oliver Twist
The Once and Future King
One Flew Over the Cuckoo's Nest
One Hundred Years of Solitude
Othello
Our Town
The Outsiders
Paradise Lost
The Pearl
The Picture of Dorian Gray
Poe's Short Stories
A Portrait of the Artist as a Young Man
Pride and Prejudice
The Prince
A Raisin in the Sun
The Red Badge of Courage
The Republic
The Return of the King
Richard III
Robinson Crusoe
Romeo and Juliet
Scarlet Letter
A Separate Peace
Silas Marner
Sir Gawain and the Green Knight
Slaughterhouse-Five
Song of Solomon
The Sound and the Fury
The Stranger
A Streetcar Named Desire
The Sun Also Rises
A Tale of Two Cities
The Taming of the Shrew
The Tempest
Tess of the d'Urbervilles
The Things They Carried
The Two Towers
Their Eyes Were Watching God
Things Fall Apart
To Kill a Mockingbird
Treasure Island
Twelfth Night
Ulysses
Uncle Tom's Cabin
Walden
War and Peace
Wuthering Heights
A Yellow Raft in Blue Water